INTERNATIONAL RELATIONS IN SOUTH ASIA

DIRECTORY OF INSTITUTIONS

INTERNATIONAL RELATIONS IN SOUTH ASIA

DIRECTORY OF INSTITUTIONS

Compiled by

GILLES BOQUÉRAT

MANOHAR

CENTRE DE SCIENCES HUMAINES

1999

Rs. 200

First published 1999

ISBN 81-7304-288-8

Published by
Ajay Kumar Jain for
Manohar Publishers & Distributors
2/6 Ansari Road, Daryaganj
New Delhi 110002

Typeset by
A J Software Publishing Co. Pvt. Ltd.
305 Durga Chambers
1333 D.B. Gupta Road
Karol Bagh, New Delhi 110005

Printed at
Rajkamal Electric Press
B 35/9 G T Karnal Road Indl Area
Delhi 110033

CONTENTS

FOREWORD

I felt the need for a directory compiling basic information on South Asian institutions working in the field of international relations when, as a research scholar based at the *Centre de Sciences Humaines* (CSH)—a French research institution located in New Delhi—, I had to identify these institutes and academic centres during my stay in India and my visits to the neighbouring countries.

My aim was to have a list of institutions as comprehensive as possible. Since international relations covers a wide range of topics, it was considered useful to include not only the traditional fields of international politics and strategic issues, but also some remarkable institutes working primarily on economics. Relevant centres of excellence, for which international relations is only one field of research among others, do also find a place in this directory. Being institution-wise, only publications published by the institution itself, or in collaboration with a publishing house, are mentioned in this directory. Originally, it was also my intention to provide more detailed information on the faculty members and research scholars whose names are hereinafter included. It turned out to be too tough a proposition for a first edition.

I would like to thank, first of all, Uma Krishnan, Publications incharge at the *Centre de Sciences Humaines*, for her logistical support after my return to Paris and her patience in sending numerous reminders to defaulting institutions (for those which have nevertheless not replied, only minimal information in our possession are given on a country-basis). My thanks also go to Dr. Bruno Dorin and Dr. Pierre Audinet, successive directors of the CSH, for making this publication possible. Lastly, many thanks to the Heads of institutions for their co-operation in answering our questionnaire.

This directory has taken a long time to compile and in spite of a regular updating, there might be some minor differences between the information I collected from the returned questionnaires and the exact position in the institutions at the time of publication (for instance, in case of rotating chairmanship, the Director or the Head of department may have changed).

This directory is meant to be regularly updated, therefore we would greatly appreciate it if the institutions could help us in this regard, by eventually completing the information appearing in the following pages. The contact address is:

The Director
Centre de Sciences Humaines
2 Aurangzeb Road
New Delhi 110011
India

I hope finally that this directory will help the interaction among South Asian scholars as well as with their colleagues from the rest of the world.

GILLES BOQUÉRAT
Centre d'Etudes
de l'Inde et
de l'Asie du Sud
Paris, June 1998

CENTRE DE SCIENCES HUMAINES (CSH)

2, AURANGZEB ROAD
NEW DELHI - 110 011
India
(91-11) 301 62 59 / 301 41 73
(91-11) 301 84 80
public@csh.ernet.in
website: http://www.france.diplomatie.fr/hote/delhi-csh/home.htm

Year of Creation
1989

Research Orientations of Institute
Through joint research programmes, the CSH's aim is to highlight the contemporary dynamics of development in South Asian countries.

Areas of Expertise
International Politics and Diplomacy, International Economics, Social Sciences and Humanities.

Regional Scope
Western Europe, South Asia.

Activities
Research Programmes (*International and regional relations from antiquity to our days*, *Economic regulation and sustainable development*, *Institutional structures and political constructions of identity*, *Culture, communication and power: the facets of modernity*, *Urban dynamics*), Conferences & Seminars, Exchange Programmes with other institutions, Library, Documentation Centre.

Publications
MONOGRAPHS: *Contributions CSH* (French/English, 1, 1996-): V. Dupont, *Spatial patterns of residence and work in Delhi with special*

reference to the location strategies of pavement dwellers (97/1); P. Audinet & E. Fages, *Energy policy options: costs for the Indian economy* (97/2); N. El Alami, S. Tawa Lama, A. Vaugier-Chatterjee & J. Zerinini, *Les élections générales d'avril 1996 et la scène politique post-électorale* (97/3); N. El Alami, *Le mouvement communiste indien et l'apprentissage de la légalité républicaine (1920-1964)* (97/4); K. Buffetrille, *Reflections on pilgrimage to sacred mountains, lakes and caves* (97/5); M.-H. Zérah, *Some issues in urban water management: household response to water supply unreliability in Delhi* (97/6); V. Dupont, *City History - Life Histories: changing equations. Migration surveys and biographical data collection in Delhi* (97/7); M.-C. Saglio, *Political mobility amongst the untouchables and caste as a political tool: the case of the Carmakars of Dharavi (Mumbai)* (97/8); D.-C. Martin, *Aesthetic transformations, collective representations and social meaning. 'The Famous Invincible Darkies', Cape Town's Coon Carnival* (98/1); P. Audinet & E. Fages, *Changement climatique et allocation des ressources du FEM: le cas de l'Inde* (98/2); A. Jobert, *La Cour suprême en Inde* (98/3); G. Boquérat, *Une lecture de l'attitude de l'Inde durant la crise du Golfe* (98/4).

BOOKS (recent publications): G. Boquérat & I.N. Mukherji, *Economic and Political Atlas of the SAARC* (1996); P. Cadène & D. Vidal (eds.), *Webs of Trade* (1997); F. De Romanis & A. Tchernia (eds.), *Crossings: Early Mediterranean Contacts with India* (1997); D.-S. Khan, *Conversions and Shifting Identities* (1997); J.M. Lafont, *Indika: Essays in Indo-French Relations (1630-1976)* (1999); H.S. Chopra, R. Frank & J. Schröder (eds.), *National Identity and Regional Cooperation* (1999).

Members

Dr. Bruno DORIN (Director and Research Fellow - Economist)
Dr. Gilles BOQUERAT (Research Fellow - Historian)
Dr. Jean-Marie LAFONT (Research Fellow - Historian)
Dr. (Ms.) Anne VAUGIER-CHATTERJEE (Research Fellow - Political Scientist)
Dr. (Ms.) Marie-Hélène ZERAH (Research Fellow - Economist)
Ms. Stéphanie TAWA LAMA (Research Fellow - Political Scientist)
Ms. Jasmine ZERININI (Research Fellow - Political Scientist)
Mr. Colin DAUDE (Research Assistant - Economist)
Ms. Elise RICADAT (Secretary General)

Ms. Gur Amrit BHALLA (Executive Assistant to Director)
Ms. Uma KRISHNAN (Publications incharge)
Ms. Preeti JHANGIANI (Librarian - Documentalist)

Affiliated Members
Dr. (Ms.) Véronique ALARY (Economist)
Dr. Pierre AUDINET (Economist)
Dr. Bernard BEL (Computer Scientist)
Dr. (Ms.) Véronique DUPONT (Demographer)

Affiliated Ph.D. Scholars
Mr. Emmanuel BON, Economist
Ms. Eric CALPAS, Sociologist
Mr. Gilles CHUYEN, Political Scientist
Ms. Marie DELPECH, Art Historian
Mr. Emmanuel GRIMAUD, Anthropologist
Mr. Emmanuel HACHE, Economist
Mr. Nicolas JAOUL, Political Scientist
Mr. Denis LISCIA, Economist
Ms. Marie LLORENTE, Economist
Ms. Frédérique PAGANI, Ethnologist
Ms. Patricia PIERONI, Economist
Ms. Isabelle SAINT-MEZARD, Political Scientist
Ms. Anoussia SARAVANE, Anthropologist
Mr. Arnaud SAULI, Historian
Mr. Dhananjay TINGAL, Geographer
Ms. Mélanie VANDENHELSKEN, Ethnologist

BANGLADESH

DHAKA

BANGLADESH INSTITUTE OF DEVELOPMENT STUDIES (BIDS)

BANGLADESH INSTITUTE OF INTERNATIONAL AND STRATEGIC STUDIES (BIISS)

BANGLADESH INSTITUTE OF LAW AND INTERNATIONAL AFFAIRS (BILIA)

CENTRE FOR DEVELOPMENT RESEARCH, BANGLADESH (CDRB)

DEPARTMENT OF INTERNATIONAL RELATIONS, UNIVERSITY OF DHAKA

CENTRE FOR POLICY DIALOGUE

DEPARTMENT OF HISTORY, UNIVERSITY OF DHAKA

DEPARTMENT OF POLITICAL SCIENCE, UNIVERSITY OF DHAKA

DEPARTMENT OF GOVERNMENT AND POLITICS, UNIVERSITY OF JAHANGIRNAGAR

CHITTAGONG

DEPARTMENT OF HISTORY, UNIVERSITY OF CHITTAGONG

DEPARTMENT OF POLITICAL SCIENCE, UNIVERSITY OF CHITTAGONG

BANGLADESH INSTITUTE OF DEVELOPMENT STUDIES (BIDS)

E-17 AGARGAON, SHER-E-BANGLA NAGAR
DHAKA - 1207
Bangladesh
(880-2) 911 69 59, 810 759
(880-2) 813 023
computer.bids@drik.bgd.toolnet.org

Year of Creation
1957

Research Orientations of Institute
Basic research on development issues and policy formulation.

Areas of Expertise
International Economics, International Trade, Population and Development, Poverty Alleviation, Industry, Agriculture and Rural Development, Population Studies, Gender, Micro-Credit.

Regional Scope
South Asia, Southeast Asia.

Activities
Research Programmes, Conferences & Seminars, Library, Documentation Centre.

Publications

JOURNALS: *The Bangladesh Development Studies* (quarterly, 1, 1973-), *Unnayan Samikhya* in vernacular (annual).

REPORTS: Series.

MONOGRAPHS: Series.

BOOKS (recent publications): Abu Abdullah (ed.), *Modernisation at Bay: Structure and Change in Bangladesh*; Rushidan Islam Rahman, *Poverty and Development: Bangladesh Perspective* (Bengali); Barbara Van Koppen & Simeen Mahmud, *Women and Water Pump in*

Bangladesh: Impact of Participation in Irrigation Groups on Women Status.

Members

Mr. Abu Ahmed ABDULLAH (Director General)
Dr. Masihur Rahman KHAN (Research Director)
Dr. Mahmudul ALAM (Senior Research Fellow)
Dr. M. ASADUZZAMAN (Senior Research Fellow)
Dr. Zaid BAKHT (Senior Research Fellow)
Dr. Omar Haider CHOWDHURY (Senior Research Fellow)
Dr. Raisul Awal MAHMOOD (Senior Research Fellow)
Dr. Khan Ahmed Syed MURSHID (Senior Research Fellow)
Dr. Md. Abul QUASEM (Senior Research Fellow)
Dr. Atiur RAHMAN (Senior Research Fellow)
Dr. Rushidan Islam RAHMAN (Senior Research Fellow)
Dr. Quazi SHAHABUDDIN (Senior Research Fellow)
Dr. (Ms.) Rita AFSAR (Research Fellow)
Dr. Chowdhury ANWARUZZAMAN (Research Fellow)
Dr. (Ms.) Anwara BEGUM (Research Fellow)
Dr. (Ms.) Sharifa BEGUM (Research Fellow)
Dr. Debapriya BHATTACHARYA (Research Fellow)
Mr. Md. Karim Ullah BHUIYAN (Research Fellow)
Dr. Osman Haider CHOWDHURY (Research Fellow)
Ms. Shamin HAMID (Research Fellow)
Mr. Kazi Zahid HOSSAIN (Research Fellow)
Dr. K.M. Nabiul ISLAM (Research Fellow)
Dr. Abdul LATIF (Research Fellow)
Dr. Sirajul Islam LASKAR (Research Fellow)
Ms. Simeen MAHMUD (Research Fellow)
Dr. (Ms.) Pratima Paul MAJUMDER (Research Fellow)
Dr. Abdul Hye MONDAL (Research Fellow)
Dr. Narayan Chandra NATH (Research Fellow)
Dr. Hossain Zillur RAHMAN (Research Fellow)
Mr. Mizanur RAHMAN (Research Fellow)
Dr. Dilip Kumar ROY (Research Fellow)
Dr. Bimal Kumar SAHA (Research Fellow)
Dr. Binayak SEN (Research Fellow)
Mr. Md. SOHAIL (Research Fellow)
Dr. Kazi Ali TOUFIQUE (Research Fellow)
Mr. Md. Salim ULLAH (Research Fellow)

Dr. Sajjad ZOHIR (Research Fellow)
Ms. Salma Chowdhury ZOHIR (Research Fellow)
Mr. Md. Kamar ALI (Research Associate)
Mr. S.M. Zulfiqar ALI (Research Associate)
Ms. Ayesha BANU (Research Associate)
Mr. Md. Abul BASHAR (Research Associate)
Mr. A.B.M. Shamsul ISLAM (Research Associate)
Dr. (Ms.) Fahmida Akter KHATUN (Research Associate)
Mr. Md. YUNUS (Research Associate)

BANGLADESH INSTITUTE OF INTERNATIONAL AND STRATEGIC STUDIES (BIISS)

1/46 ELEPHANT ROAD
DHAKA - 1000
Bangladesh
(880-2) 406 234, 411 267, 406 245, 412 693
(880-2) 832 625
biiss@drik.bgd.toolnet.org
website: http://www.bangla.net/webera/biiss

Year of Creation
1978

Research Orientations of Institute
The objective of the Institute is to conduct and promote independant research and dissemination of objective knowledge in the fields of international relations, foreign policy and security, with particular relevance to Bangladesh. Its aim is also to function as a forum for debate and deliberation by scholars, decision-makers and members of various professional groups aimed at greater public understanding of national, regional and international problems and events.

Areas of Expertise
International Politics and Diplomacy, Defence and Strategic Studies, International Economics, International Law, Development issues.

Regional Scope
Western Europe, Russia (+ Eastern Europe), North America, Africa, West Asia, Central Asia, South Asia, Southeast Asia, East Asia, Southwest Pacific.

Activities
Research Programmes, Conferences & Seminars, Library, Documentation Centre, Institutional linkages with several similar academic and research institutions both within and beyond South Asia.

Publications

JOURNALS: *BIISS Quarterly Journal* (1, 1980-), *Bangladesh Foreign Policy Survey* (quarterly, 1, 1995-).

MONOGRAPHS: *BIISS papers* (no. 13: Environmental Challenges to Bangladesh (1991), no. 14: The Gulf War and "The New World Order": Implications for the Third World (1992), no. 15: Challenges of Governance in India: Fundamentals under Threat (1995), no. 16: Bangladesh in United Nations Peacekeeping Operations (1998).

REPORTS: *Regional Press Digest* (monthly)

BOOKS (recent publications): *Bangladesh and SAARC: Issues, Perspectives and Outlook; Bangladesh: Society, Polity and Economy; South Asia's Security: Primacy of Internal Dimension.*

Members

Brigadier Muhammad Shahedul Anam KHAN (Director General)
Col. Emdaduddin AHMED (Director)
Dr. IFTEKHARUZZAMAN (Research Director - on lien abroad)
Dr. Abdur Rob KHAN (Research Director)
Dr. (Ms.) Shaheen AFROZE (Senior Research Fellow)
Mr. Mohammed Humayun KABIR (Senior Research Fellow)
Mr. Mizanur Rahman KHAN (Senior Research Fellow)
Mr. A.K.M. Abdus SABUR (Senior Research Fellow)
Dr. Abul Kalam AZAD (Research Fellow)
Mrs. Nahid ISLAM (Research Fellow)
Mr. Shamsur RAHMAN (Research Fellow)
Mr. Abu Taher SALAHUDDIN AHMED (Research Fellow)
Mr. Sabbir AHMED (Research Associate)
Ms. Neila HUSAIN (Research Associate)
Mr. Md. Shamsul ISLAM (Research Associate)
Mr. Habibur Rahman KHAN (Research Associate)
Mr. Yunus Ali SHEIKH (Research Associate)
Mrs. Saleha SULTANA (Deputy Director, Library and Documentation)

BANGLADESH INSTITUTE OF LAW AND INTERNATIONAL AFFAIRS (BILIA)

✉ HOUSE NO. 22, ROAD NO. 07
DHANMONDI R/A
DHAKA - 1205
Bangladesh
☎ (880-2) 911 17 18
(880-2) 326 303
bilia@citechco.net

Year of Creation
1972

Areas of Expertise
International Politics and Relations, International Law, Regional and International Economics.

Regional Scope
South Asia.

Activities
Research Programmes, Conferences & Seminars, Exchange Programmes with other institutions, Library.

Publications

JOURNALS: *Journal of International Affairs* (bi-annual, 1, 1994-), *Bangladesh Journal of Law* (bi-annual, 1, 1997-).

REPORTS: *Bangladesh Supreme Court Reports* (quarterly, 1, 1976-).

BOOKS (recent publications): F.K.M.A. Munim, *Legal Aspects of Martial Law* (1989); Selina Haq & Ehsanul Haque, *Disintegrative Process in Action: The Case of South Asia* (1990); Hameda Hossain, Roushan Jahan & Salma Sobhan, *No Better Option ? Industrial Women Workers in Bangladesh* (1990); Mahmudul Islam, *Constitutional Law of Bangladesh* (1995).

Members

Mr. Wahin RAHMAN (Director)
Mr. Masud MANNAN (Senior Research Fellow)
Ms. Rabeya RAHMAN (Senior Research Fellow)
Ms. Shakila F. RAHMAN (Research Fellow)
Ms. Seema HAIDER CHOWDHURY (Research Associate)
Mr. Abdul GHANI KHANDKER (Librarian)

CENTRE FOR DEVELOPMENT RESEARCH, BANGLADESH (CDRB)

55, DHANMONDHI R/A, ROAD NO. 8-A
DHAKA - 1209
Bangladesh
(880-2) 811 877, 815 463
(880-2) 817 277
cdrb@agni.com

Year of Creation
1982

Areas of Expertise
International Politics and Diplomacy, International Economics.

Regional Scope
Western Europe, Russia (+ Eastern Europe), North America, South Asia, Southeast Asia, East Asia.

Activities
Research Programmes, Conferences & Seminars, Exchange Programmes with other institutions, Library, Documentation Centre.

Publications
JOURNAL: *Asian Affairs* (quarterly, 1, 1980-).

MONOGRAPHS: Occasional Papers.

Member
Dr. Mizanur Rahman SHELLEY (Chairman)

DEPARTMENT OF INTERNATIONAL RELATIONS
UNIVERSITY OF DHAKA

DHAKA - 1000
Bangladesh
(880-2) 505 769
(880-2) 865 583
ducc@agni.com

Year of Creation
1947

Research Orientations of Institute
Advanced International Relations Theory, International Political Economy, International Security and various area studies.

Areas of Expertise
International Politics and Diplomacy, Defence and Strategic Studies, International Economics, International Law.

Regional Scope
Western Europe, Russia (+ Eastern Europe), Latin America, North America, Africa (mainly Sub-Saharan Africa), Central Asia, South Asia, Southeast Asia, East Asia, Southwest Pacific.

Activities
Research Programmes (at M.Phil. and Ph.D. levels), Conferences & Seminars (occasionally jointly with *Bangladesh Institute of International and Strategic Studies*), Library (with specialized literature on International and U.N. Affairs).

Publications
JOURNALS: *Journal of International Relations* (bi-annual, 1, 1993-).

REPORTS: Occasionally.

Members
Dr. (Mrs.) Meghna GUHATHAKURTA (Chairperson & Associate Professor)

Dr. C.R. ABRAR (Professor)
Dr. Md. Ramjul HAQ (Professor)
Dr. Akmal HUSSAIN (Professor)
Dr. Muhammad SHAHIDUZZAMAN (Professor)
Dr. Shamsul Islam KHAN (Associate Professor, on lien abroad)
Dr. (Mrs.) Amena MOHSIN (Associate Professor)
Mr. Muhammad Azher Zafar SHAH (Assistant Professor)
Mr. Md. NURUZZAMAN (Lecturer)

DEPARTMENT OF HISTORY
UNIVERSITY OF CHITTAGONG

✉ CHITTAGONG 4331
Bangladesh

Year of Creation
1968

Areas of Expertise
International Politics and Diplomacy, Defence and Strategic Studies, International Law.

Regional Scope
Western Europe, Russia (+ Eastern Europe), North America, West Asia, Central Asia, South Asia, Southeast Asia, East Asia.

Activities
Research Programmes (at M.Phil. and Ph.D. levels), Conferences & Seminars.

Publications
JOURNAL: *Ithas Patrika* (Journal of History) (1, 1974-).

Members
Dr. Mahmudul HUQUE (Director)
Dr. A.M.M. Saifussin KHALED (Professor)

DEPARTMENT OF POLITICAL SCIENCE
UNIVERSITY OF CHITTAGONG

✉ CHITTAGONG 4331
Bangladesh
☎ PABX 682 031-40, 714 923 Ext. 4280
(880-31) 682 030

Research Orientations of Institute
Regional cooperation and Inter-State relations in South Asia.

Areas of Expertise
International Politics and Diplomacy.

Regional Scope
South Asia.

Activities
Research Programmes, Conferences & Seminars (organised by the *Department of Political Science* and the *Bangladesh Political Science Association*), Library.

Publications
JOURNAL: *Bangladesh Political Studies* (annual, 1, 1978-).

Members
Dr. Md. Abdur RASHID (Chairman & Professor)
Dr. Benu BARUA (Professor)
Dr. Muhammad SHAMSUDDIN (Professor)
Dr. Mokhdum-e-Mulk MUSHRAFI (Professor)
Dr. Bhuyan KABIR (Associate Professor)
Mr. Khairul ISLAM (Lecturer)

OTHER INSTITUTIONS

CENTRE FOR POLICY DIALOGUE
6 A ESKATON GARDEN ROAD
DHAKA - 1000 (Bangladesh)

DEPARTMENT OF HISTORY,
UNIVERSITY OF DHAKA
RAMNA
DHAKA - 1000 (Bangladesh)

DEPARTMENT OF POLITICAL SCIENCE,
UNIVERSITY OF DHAKA
RAMNA
DHAKA - 1000 (Bangladesh)

DEPARTMENT OF GOVERNMENT AND POLITICS,
UNIVERSITY OF JAHANGIRNAGAR
SAVAR
DHAKA - 1000 (Bangladesh)

INDIA

NEW DELHI

*ACADEMY OF THIRD WORLD STUDIES,
JAMIA MILLIA ISLAMIA*

CENTRE FOR PEACE STUDIES

CENTRE FOR POLICY RESEARCH (CPR)

CENTRE FOR THE STUDY OF DEVELOPING SOCIETIES (CSDS)
- *THE INSTITUTE OF CHINESE STUDIES*
- *THE INSTITUTE OF PEACE AND CONFLICT STUDIES (IPCS)*

*DEPARTMENT OF POLITICAL SCIENCE,
DELHI UNIVERSITY*

INDIAN COUNCIL FOR RESEARCH ON INTERNATIONAL ECONOMIC RELATIONS (ICRIER)

INDIAN COUNCIL OF WORLD AFFAIRS (ICWA)

INSTITUTE FOR DEFENCE STUDIES AND ANALYSES (IDSA)

INDIAN INSTITUTE OF FOREIGN TRADE (IIFT)

RESEARCH AND INFORMATION SYSTEM FOR THE NON-ALIGNED AND OTHER DEVELOPING COUNTRIES (RIS)

*SCHOOL OF INTERNATIONAL STUDIÈS (SIS),
JAWAHARLAL NEHRU UNIVERSITY :*
- *CENTRE FOR AMERICAN AND WEST EUROPEAN STUDIES*
- *CENTRE FOR DIPLOMACY, INTERNATIONAL LAW & ECONOMICS*
- *CENTRE FOR EAST ASIAN STUDIES*
- *CENTRE FOR INTERNATIONAL POLITICS,*

ORGANIZATION & DISARMAMENT
- *CENTRE FOR RUSSIAN, CENTRAL ASIAN & EAST EUROPEAN STUDIES*
- *CENTRE FOR SOUTH, CENTRAL, SOUTHEAST ASIAN & SOUTHWEST PACIFIC STUDIES*
- *CENTRE FOR WEST ASIAN AND AFRICAN STUDIES*

SOUTH ASIAN CENTRE FOR STRATEGIC STUDIES (SACSS)

DEPARTMENT OF CHINESE AND JAPANESE STUDIES, UNIVERSITY OF DELHI

ALIGARH

CENTRE FOR STRATEGIC STUDIES, ALIGARH MUSLIM UNIVERSITY

CENTRE OF WEST ASIAN STUDIES, ALIGARH MUSLIM UNIVERSITY

CALCUTTA

DEPARTMENT OF INTERNATIONAL RELATIONS, JADAVPUR UNIVERSITY

DEPARTMENT OF SOUTH AND SOUTHEAST ASIAN STUDIES, UNIVERSITY OF CALCUTTA

MAULANA ABDUL KALAM AZAD INSTITUTE OF ASIAN STUDIES

CHANDIGARH

CENTRE FOR THE STUDY OF GEOPOLITICS, DEPARTMENT OF POLITICAL SCIENCE, PUNJAB UNIVERSITY

CHENNAI

DEPARTMENT OF DEFENCE STUDIES, UNIVERSITY OF CHENNAI

CENTRE FOR SOUTH AND SOUTHEAST ASIAN STUDIES, UNIVERSITY OF CHENNAI

GOA

CENTRE FOR LATIN AMERICAN STUDIES,
UNIVERSITY OF GOA

HYDERABAD

CENTRE FOR AREA STUDIES (URBAN DEVELOPMENT AND REGIONAL PLANNING IN THE INDIAN OCEAN REGION)

DEPARTMENT OF POLITICAL SCIENCE,
UNIVERSITY OF HYDERABAD

JAIPUR

SOUTH ASIA STUDIES CENTRE (SASC),
UNIVERSITY OF RAJASTHAN

MUMBAI

CENTRE FOR CENTRAL EURASIAN STUDIES,
UNIVERSITY OF MUMBAI

CENTRE FOR AFRICAN STUDIES,
UNIVERSITY OF MUMBAI

PONDICHERRY

SCHOOL OF INTERNATIONAL STUDIES,
UNIVERSITY OF PONDICHERRY

PUNE

DEPARTMENT OF DEFENCE AND STRATEGIC STUDIES,
UNIVERSITY OF POONA

SRINAGAR

CENTRE OF CENTRAL ASIAN STUDIES (CCAS),
UNIVERSITY OF KASHMIR

TIRUPATI

CENTRE FOR STUDIES ON INDOCHINA, SRI VENKATESHWARA UNIVERSITY

VARANASI

CENTRE FOR THE STUDY OF NEPAL, BENARES HINDU UNIVERSITY

VISAKHAPATNAM

CENTRE FOR SOUTH ASIAN STUDIES, COLLEGE OF ARTS, COMMERCE AND LAW ANDHRA UNIVERSITY

ACADEMY OF THIRD WORLD STUDIES
JAMIA MILLIA ISLAMIA

JAMIA NAGAR
NEW DELHI - 110025
India
(91-11) 684 44 38
(91-11) 682 12 32

Year of Creation
1988

Research Orientations of Institute
Socio-economic developmental problems of the Third World.

Areas of Expertise
International Politics and Diplomacy, Defence and Strategic Studies, International Economics, Environmental Regeneration.

Regional Scope
Latin America, Africa, West Asia, Central Asia, South Asia, Southeast Asia, East Asia.

Activities
Research Programmes, Conferences & Seminars, Exchange Programmes with other institutions, Library, Documentation Centre.

Publications
REPORTS: Occasionally.

MONOGRAPHS: *Occasional Paper Series.*

Members
Dr. Z.H. ZAIDI (Honorary Director & Professor)
Dr. Shri PRAKASH (Professor)

Dr. (Ms.) Vanita RAY (Reader)
Dr. Asad RIZVI (Lecturer)
Dr. (Ms.) Sabiah ALAM (Research Associate)
Dr. (Ms.) Safia MEHDI (Research Associate)
Dr. Subodh NARAIN MALAKAR (Research Associate)

CENTRE FOR PEACE STUDIES

A-39 SOUTH EXTENSION - I
NEW DELHI - 110 049
India
(91-11) 469 88 86
(91-11) 464 99 96
cpsnd@del2.vsnl.net.in

Year of Creation
1993

Research Orientations of Institute
Researches conducted in the areas of peace, conflict resolution, rise of religious fundamentalism, and international politics.

Areas of Expertise
International Politics and Diplomacy, Defence and Strategic Studies, International Law.

Regional Scope
Western Europe, Russia (+ Eastern Europe), North America, Africa, West Asia, Central Asia, South Asia, Southeast Asia, East Asia.

Activities
Research Programmes, Conferences & Seminars, Documentation Centre.

Publications
JOURNAL: *Journal of Peace Studies* (bi-monthly, 1, 1993-)

REPORTS: Occasionally.

MONOGRAPHS: Occasionally.

Members
Dr. Riyaz PUNJABI (Director & Professor)
Dr. Saleem KIDWAI (Coordinator, Research programmes)

Dr. Ashok K. BEHURIA (Assistant Director)
Dr. Momin JAAN (Research Associate)
Dr. Amitabh MATTOO (Research Associate)
Dr. A.K. PASHA (Member, Research Board)

CENTRE FOR POLICY RESEARCH (CPR)

DHARMAMARG, CHANAKYAPURI
NEW DELHI - 110 021
India
☎ (91-11) 611 52 73-76
(91-11) 687 27 46
cpr@giasdl01.vsnl.net.in
website: http://www.cprindia.com

Year of Creation
1973

Research Orientations of Institute
A leading policy think tank of India, CPR is designed to promote highly focussed research on various national and international, social, economic and political issues.

Areas of Expertise
International Politics and Diplomacy, Defence and Strategic Studies, International Economics.

Regional Scope
Russia (+ Eastern Europe), North America, West Asia, Central Asia, South Asia, Southeast Asia, East Asia.

Activities
Research Programmes, Conferences & Seminars, Exchange Programmes with other institutions, Library, Documentation Centre.

Publications
REPORTS: *CPR Quarterly Report.*

MONOGRAPHS (recent publications) : V.A. Pai Panandiker, *Population Growth and Economic Development* (1995); P.R. Chari, N. Chadha & M. Raza, *Confidence-Building Measures in South Asia* (1995); Maroof Raza, *Civil-Military Relations in India and Pakistan* (1995); R. & K. Gulhati, V. Nagar & S. Subramaniam, *Improving Voluntary Work in India* (1995); L.P. Singh, *Office of Prime Minister: Retrospect and Prospect* (1995); Centre for Policy Research: *Indo-Bangladesh Dialogue: Economic and Trade Cooperation* (1995); B. Chellaney, *US Counterproliferation Initiatives: Issues and Implications* (1996); S.L. Rao, *Report of the First Meeting of the Indian Ocean Research Network* (1996); Ramaswamy R. Iyer, *The Cauvery Dispute* (1996); G.G. Christo, *The Privatisation and Pricing of Professional Education* (1996); V.A. Pai Panandiker, *Demography, Democracy and Development* (1996); E. Sridharan, *Coalition Politics in India: Lessons from Theory, Comparison and Recent History* (1997); E. Sridharan, *Duverger's Law, Its Re-formulations and the Evolution of the Indian Party System* (1997); E. Sridharan, *Political Institutions and Economic Reform: Lessons from the Indian Experience 1991-96* (1997), E. Sridharan, *Towards Collective Action for State Funding of Elections ?* (1997); K.C. Sivaramakrishnan, *Under Franchise in Urban Areas* (1997).

BOOKS (recent publication): P.D. Malgavkar, *Population Stabilisation: Identification of Factors Responsible for Population Stabilisation and Delineation of Policy Initiatives* (1997).

Members

Dr. V.A. PAI PANANDIKER (President)
Mr. Rajmohan GANDHI (Research Professor)
Mr. Ramaswamy Rajagopal IYER (Research Professor)
Mr. Bharat KARNAD (Research Professor)
Mr. Ved MARWAH (Research Professor)
Mr. K.C. SIVARAMAKRISHNAN (Research Professor)
Mr. Boobli George VERGHESE (Research Professor)
Dr. Charan WADHVA (Research Professor)
Dr. (Ms.) Navnita CHADHA-BEHERA (Assistant Research Professor)
Dr. Gulshan SACHDEVA (Assistant Research Professor)
Dr. Eswaran SRIDHARAN (Assistant Research Professor)
Dr. Brahma CHELLANEY (Research Fellow)
Mr. Pran CHOPRA (Visiting Professor)
Dr. Kaval GULHATI (Visiting Professor)
Mr. Pavagada Venkata INDIRESAN (Visiting Professor)
Dr. Subash C. KASHYAP (Honorary Visiting Professor)
Mr. P.D. MALGAVKAR (Visiting Professor)
Dr. Sharad S. MARATHE (Honorary Visiting Professor)
Dr. Ajit MOZOOMDAR (Visiting Professor)

Mr. N.K. MUKARJI (Visiting Professor)
Gen. G.F. RODRIGUES (Retd.) (Honorary Visiting Professor)
Mr. Ayilam P. VENKATESWARAN (Visiting Professor)
Mr. Sanjoy HAZARIKA (Senior Fellow)
Dr. Ajay K. MEHRA (Visiting Fellow)
Dr. O.P. SHARMA (Visiting Fellow)
Dr. Ramgopal MISRA (Consultant)

CENTRE FOR THE STUDY OF DEVELOPING SOCIETIES (CSDS)

29, RAJPUR ROAD
DELHI - 110 054
India
(91-11) 252 11 51, 294 21 99
(91-11) 294 34 50
csds@del2.vsnl.net.in

Year of Creation
1963

Research Orientations of Institute
The CSDS has four main focii: democratic politics and its future; politics of culture and politics of knowledge; politics of alternatives and human futures; and violence, ethnicity and diversity.

Areas of Expertise
International Politics and Diplomacy, Political Science.

Regional Scope
Western Europe, North America, South Asia, East Asia.

Activities
Research Programmes, Conferences & Seminars, Exchange Programmes with other institutions, Library, Documentation Centre.

Publications
JOURNAL: *Alternatives* (quarterly, 1, 1975 -).

Members
Dr. V.B. SINGH (Director; Electoral Studies, Party System, Ethnic Politics)
Ms. Madhu KISHWAR (History of Social Reforms, Gender)
Mr. Gopal KRISHNA (Honorary Fellow; Political History, Islamic Studies)
Ms. Nivedita MENON (Political Theory, Gender, Human Rights)

Mr. D.R. NAGRAJ (Honorary Fellow; Literary Theory, Politics of Cultural Choices)
Mr. Ashis NANDY (Political Psychology, Future Studies, Sociology of Knowledge, Popular Culture)
Ms. Chandrika PARMAR (Secretary to the Centre; Political Theory, Political Culture, Electoral Studies)
Mr. Ramashray ROY (Honorary Fellow ; Political Theory, Alternative Development)
Mr. Suresh SHARMA (Social History, Development Alternatives)
Mr. D.L. SHETH (Editor, *Alternatives*, Political Sociology, Social Movements, Human Rights)
Mr. R.K. SRIVASTAVA (Social Movements, Development Alternatives)
Mr. Ravi VASUDEVAN (Media Studies, Popular Culture)
Mr. Shiv VISVANATHAN (Sociology of Science, Semiotics, Anthropology of Corruption)
Mr. Yogendra YADAV (Political Theory, Democracy, Electoral Politics)

THE INSTITUTE OF CHINESE STUDIES

9, BHAGWANDAS ROAD
NEW DELHI - 110 002
India
☎ 4 (91-11) 338 81 55

Research Orientations of Institute
The Institute of Chinese Studies promotes multidisciplinary research on political, social, scientific and military affairs in China and China's relations with its neighbours.

Areas of Expertise
International Politics and Diplomacy, Defence and Strategic Studies.

Regional Scope
East Asia.

Activities
Research Programmes, Conferences & Seminars, Documentation Centre.

Publications
JOURNAL: *China Report* (quarterly, 1, 1964-).

MONOGRAPHS: Seminar series.

Members
Dr. G.D. DESHINGKAR (Director; Security Studies, Science and Technology)
Ms. Mira Sinha BHATTACHARJEA (Contemporary Politics)
Mr. Tan CHUNG (History and Culture)
Dr. G.P. DESHPANDE (Professor, Foreign Policy)
Mr. Vinod KHANNA (Policy Studies)
Dr. Manoranjan MOHANTY (Editor, *China Report*, Contemporary Politics, Ideology)

Mr. C.V. RANGANATHAN (India-China Relations)
Dr. Satish SABHARWAL (Professor, Society and History)
Ms. Patricia UBEROI (Gender Studies, Social Reforms)
Mr. Huang I-SHU (Literature)

THE INSTITUTE OF PEACE AND CONFLICT STUDIES (IPCS)

11, VASANT ENCLAVE
NEW DELHI - 110 057
India
☎ (91-11) 615 20 09, 614 24 58
(91-11) 614 24 58
ipcs@del2.vsnl.net.in
website: http://www.southernasia.com/ipcs

Year of Creation
1996

Research Orientations of Institute
The objective of the Institute is to discern alternate approaches to security relevant to India and the world. The Institute examines a broad range of issues and security questions to promote a harmonious and secure regional and global environment. Whilst conventional and nuclear security issues are not neglected, the emphasis is on addressing the internal and non-military dimensions of security.

Areas of Expertise
International Politics and Diplomacy, Defence and Strategic Studies.

Regional Scope
Western Europe, Russia (+ Eastern Europe), North America, Central Asia, South Asia, Southeast Asia, East Asia.

Activities
Research Programmes, Conferences & Seminars, Library, Documentation Centre, Website and online debate on South Asian security affairs.

Publications
JOURNAL: Newsletter.

MONOGRAPHS: Occasionally.

Members

Maj. Gen. (Retd.) Dipankar BANERJEE (Co-Director)
Mr. P. Ranga CHARI (Co-Director)
Dr. Vidya Shankar AIYAR (Research Officer)
Ms. A. Mallika JOSEPH (Research Officer)
Mr. Arpit RAJAIN (Research Officer)

DEPARTMENT OF POLITICAL SCIENCE DELHI UNIVERSITY

✉ FACULTY OF ARTS, EXTENSION BUILDING,
DELHI UNIVERSITY
DELHI - 110 007
India
☎ (91-11) 725 77 25, extn. 214
(91-11) 725 73 36

Year of Creation
1955

Research Orientations of Institute
Political Theory, Politics of Developing Countries, Indian Politics.

Areas of Expertise
International Politics and Diplomacy, Defence and Strategic Studies, International Law.

Regional Scope
Western Europe, Russia (+ Eastern Europe), Latin America, North America, Africa, West Asia, South Asia, Southeast Asia, East Asia.

Activities
Research Programmes, Conferences & Seminars, Library, Documentation Centre.

Publications
JOURNAL: Newsletter.

REPORTS: *11th Lok Sabha Elections.*

Members
Dr. Subroto MUKHERJEE (Head of Department & Professor)
Dr. (Ms.) Noorjehan BAWA (Professor)
Dr. (Ms.) Neera CHANDOK (Professor)
Dr. S.K. CHAUBE (Professor)

Dr. R.B. JAIN (Professor)
Dr. (Ms.) Susheela KAUSHIK (Professor)
Dr. Mahendra KUMAR (Professor)
Dr. Manoranjan MOHANTY (Professor)
Dr. M.P. SINGH (Professor)
Dr. B.B. SIRCAR (Professor)
Dr. Bidyut CHAKRAVARTHY (Associate Professor)
Dr. (Ms.) Veena KUKRAJA (Associate Professor)
Dr. (Ms.) Shantha VERMA (Associate Professor)

INDIAN COUNCIL FOR RESEARCH ON INTERNATIONAL ECONOMIC RELATIONS (ICRIER)

INDIA HABITAT CENTRE
CORE VI-A, 4th Floor
NEW DELHI - 110 003
India
(91-11) 469 20 70, 464 52 18-20
(91-11) 462 01 80
root@icrier.ren.nic.in

Year of Creation
1982

Areas of Expertise
International Economics, Area Studies.

Regional Scope
Western Europe, Russia (+ Eastern Europe), North America, Africa, South Asia, Southeast Asia, East Asia, Southwest Pacific.

Activities
Research Programmes, Conferences & Seminars, Exchange Programmes with other institutions, Library, Documentation Centre.

Publications
MONOGRAPHS (recent publications): R.L. Chawla (ed.), *Development Cooperation for Strengthening International Economic Relations: India, Germany, EC and Japan* (1992); Jeffrey Sachs, *India's Unfinished Reform Agenda* (1994); Wing Thye Woo, *Dynamic Growth in China: Lessons in Economic Reform for Other Developing Economies* (1994); Andrew Mason, *Population, Development and Demographic Freedom* (1995); Ronald I. Mckinnon, *Economic Liberalization and Financial Reforms in India: An Outsider's Perspective* (1995); S.P. Gupta & R.L. Chawla (eds.), *Prospects of FDI in Post Liberalization Era* (1995).

Members

Dr. (Ms.) Isher Judge AHLUWALIA (Director & Chief Executive)
Dr. (Ms.) Benu SCHNEIDER (Professor)
Dr. Pradeep SRIVASTAVA (Professor)
Dr. Sanjay AMBATKAR (Fellow)
Ms. Nisha TANEJA (Fellow)
Mr. C. Niranjan RAO (Associate Fellow)

INDIAN COUNCIL OF WORLD AFFAIRS (ICWA)

SAPRU HOUSE, BARAKHAMBA ROAD
NEW DELHI - 110 001
India
☎ (91-11) 331 90 55
Fax (91-11) 331 12 08

Year of Creation
1943

Research Orientations of Institute
Research on foreign policy issues and analytical studies of topics like upsurge of terrorism, human rights, UN and the new world order, etc. The ICWA also covers topics concerning United Nations, international institutions and UN specialised agencies.

Areas of Expertise
International Politics and Diplomacy, Defence and Strategic Studies.

Regional Scope
Western Europe, Russia (+ Eastern Europe), Latin America, North America, Africa, West Asia, Central Asia, South Asia, Southeast Asia, East Asia, Southwest Pacific.

Activities
Research Programmes, Conferences & Seminars, Library, Documentation Centre.

Publications
JOURNAL: *India Quarterly* (1, 1945-).
REPORTS: *Foreign Affairs Reports* (monthly).

Member
Dr. Harcharan Singh JOSH (Director)

INSTITUTE FOR DEFENCE STUDIES AND ANALYSES (IDSA)

BLOCK NO. 1
OLD J.N.U. CAMPUS
NEW DELHI - 110 067
India
☎ (91-11) 618 66 62, 618 75 11
4 (91-11) 618 90 23
postmast@idsa.delnet.ernet.in
idsa@giasdl01.vsnl.net.in
website: http://www.idsa-india.org

Year of Creation
1965

Research Orientations of Institute
India's national security and the impact of defence related issues on the economic and social spheres. Military and methods of warfare. Different orientations to defence. Disarmament. International relations, especially India's relations with its neighbours.

Areas of Expertise
International Politics and Diplomacy, Defence and Strategic Studies.

Regional Scope
Western Europe, Russia (+ Eastern Europe), Latin America, North America, Africa, West Asia, Central Asia, South Asia, Southeast Asia, East Asia, Southwest Pacific.

Activities
Research Programmes, Conferences & Seminars, Exchange Programmes with other institutions, Library, Documentation Centre.

Publications
JOURNALS: *Strategic Analysis* (monthly, 1, 1978-); *Strategic Digest* (monthly, 1, 1971-); *Asian Strategic Review* (annual, 1, 1991/92-); *News Reviews on the Americas*, *News Reviews on CIS/Russia*, *News Reviews on East Asia*; *News Reviews on South Asia and the Indian*

Ocean, *News Reviews on Southeast Asia and Australasia*; *News Reviews on West Asia* (all monthly).

REPORTS: *Light Weapons and Militancy in the Northeast*; *Light Weapons and Militancy in Sri Lanka.*

MONOGRAPHS (recent publications): *Occasional Paper Series:* Russian Military Doctrine in Transition, Defence in Indo-US Relations; *Delhi Paper Series*: Post-Cold War Pacific Asian Security - Indian Perceptions and Options, Ethno-Nationalism in Pakistan, The People's Liberation Army: Evolving Dynamics.

BOOKS (recent publications): Maj. Gen. D. Banerjee, ed., *Security in the New World Order - An Indo-French Dialogue*; *Towards an Era of Cooperation - An Indo-Australian Dialogue*; Jasjit Singh, ed., *Maritime Security*; *India-China and Panchsheel*; *South Africa-India Strategic Partnership onto the 21st Century.*

Members

Air Commodore Jasjit SINGH (Director)
Cmde C.U. BHASKAR (Deputy Director)
Dr. Jyotsna BAKSHI (Research Fellow)
Ms. Ruchita BERI (Research Fellow)
Ms. S. Ray DADWAL (Research Officer)
Ms. Sanjana JOSHI (Research Officer)
AVM K. KAK (Senior Fellow)
Ms. Tara KARTHA (Research Fellow)
Ms. Sumita KUMAR (Research Officer)
Dr. C. MAHAPATRA (Research Fellow)
Dr. O.N. MEHROTRA (Senior Fellow)
Shri D.R. MOHANTI (Associate Fellow)
Dr. G.V.C. NAIDU (Research Fellow)
Ms. Farah NAAZ (Associate Fellow)
Ms. G. PADMAJA (Associate Fellow)
Shri Rajiv NAYAN (Research Officer)
Shri A.K. PANDEY (Senior Fellow)
Dr. Savita PANDE (Research Fellow)
Shri R. RAJAGOPALAN (Research Fellow)
Shri M.V. RAPPAI (Research Fellow)
Dr. K.N. RAMACHANDRAN (Research Associate)
Shri. T.S. RAO (Senior Fellow)

Shri R. ROY-CHOUDHURY (Research Fellow)
Ms. Manpreet SETHI (Assistant Editor)
Dr. P.B. SINHA (Research Associate)
Brig. Satbir SINGH (Senior Fellow)
Dr. Swaran SINGH (Research Fellow)
Dr. Udai Bhanu SINGH (Research Fellow)
Shri. P. STOBDAN (Research Fellow)
Dr. R.R. SUBRAMANIAN (Senior Research Associate)
Ms. Sangeeta THAPLIYAL (Research Officer)
Air Cmdre S.P. TYAGI (Senior Fellow)

INDIAN INSTITUTE OF FOREIGN TRADE (IIFT)

B-21 QUTUB INSTITUTIONAL AREA
NEW DELHI - 110 016
India
(91-11) 696 38 80, 696 51 24, 696 50 51,
696 75 58, 696 53 00, 696 65 44
(91-11) 685 39 56, 686 78 41
Sprintmail ID: iift.delhi@sml.sprintrpg.ems.vsnl.net.in
VSNL ID: iift@giasdl0.vsnl.net.in

Year of Creation
1964

Research Orientations of Institute
The Institute is engaged in a variety of training and research activities which fall under the four following categories: training of export management personnel, market surveys in India and abroad, studies on various functional areas of foreign trade and provision of consultancy service in the area of international trade policy and international business.

Areas of Expertise
International Economics.

Regional Scope
Global, with a specific focus on SAARC and ASEAN.

Activities
Masters Programme in International Trade, Consultancy.

Publications
JOURNALS: *Foreign Trade Review* (quarterly, 1, 1966-), *Foreign Trade Trends and Tidings* (monthly).

REPORTS: Occasionally.

MONOGRAPHS: *Occasional Papers Series*: Competing for the Indian

Market: Local Firms vs.MNCs (1996); Foreign Direct Investment in India: Fact and Issues (1996); Regional Trade Enhancement: SAPTA and Beyond (1996); Towards Economic Integration through Regional Trade Blocs (1996); Duty Free Access to India within SAPTA Framework (1996); India's Trade Liberalisation since 1991 - A Statistical Appraisal (1996); Indian Garments Industry in the Post-MFA Period (1997); Impact of Economic Reforms on India's Major Exports - Policy Guidelines (1997); Intellectual Property Rights in the Present Indian Context (1997).

BOOKS: *Electronics Commerce* (1997); *Global Competitiveness of Indian Industries* (1997); *Global Economic Challenges in the New Millennium - India's Strategic Agenda* (1997); *India - Asean Trade Cooperation and Investment Opportunities* (1996).

Members

Dr. P.L. Sanjeev REDDY (Director General)
Dr. B. BHATTACHARYA (Dean - Research & Professor)
Dr. Brij MOHAN (Dean - Training & Professor)
Dr. A.K. SENGUPTA (Dean - Training & Professor)

RESEARCH AND INFORMATION SYSTEM FOR THE NON-ALIGNED AND OTHER DEVELOPING COUNTRIES (RIS)

ZONE IV, FOURTH FLOOR, INDIA HABITAT CENTRE,
LODHI ROAD,
NEW DELHI - 110 003
India
☎ (91-11) 461 71 36, 461 74 03, 461 77 09,
469 85 83, 462 85 09
(91-11) 462 80 68
panchmukh@giasdl01.vsnl.net.in

Year of Creation
1984

Research Orientations of Institute
RIS is a forum essentially for providing analytical support to the developing countries on the various international economic issues of concern to the process of their development. Its aims and objectives include, inter alia, promotion of the concept of self-reliance among the non-aligned and other developing countries and forging and maintaining a system of effective links amongst the various research institutions of these countries with a view to utilising their research capabilities for the maximum common benefits.

Areas of Expertise
International Economics.

Regional Scope
Western Europe, Russia (+ Eastern Europe), Latin America, North America, Africa, West Asia, Central Asia, South Asia, Southeast Asia, East Asia, Southwest Pacific.

Activities
Research Programmes, Conferences & Seminars, Exchange Programmes with other institutions, Library, Documentation Centre.

Publications

JOURNALS: *RIS Digest* (quarterly, 1, 1984-), *Biotechnology Development Review* (in collaboration with *Biotech Consortium India Ltd.*, New Delhi).

MONOGRAPHS (recent occasional papers): V.L. Rao & R. Upendra Das, *India and ASEAN: Issues in Sectoral Dialogue Partnership* (1993); Rajesh Mehta, *Single European Market and India's Trade: A Macroeconomic Analysis* (1993); Biswajit Dhar, *External Debt Crisis of Developing Countries: Its Emergence and Prospects* (1993); V.R. Panchamukhi, *Recent Developments in Trade Theory and Practice* (1994); Nagesh Kumar & Sundeep Waslekar, *Developing Countries in the International Division of Labour in Design Engineering and Construction Services: The Case of India* (1994); Ajit Singh, *How East Asia Grew So Fast? Slow Progress Towards an Analytical Consensus* (1995); Percy S. Mistry, *Regional Integration and Development: Panacea or Pitfalls* (1995); Bisjawit Dhar, *The Uruguay Round Agreement - A Critical Appraisal* (1995); Azizul Islam, *Mobilization of Domestic Financial Resources for Development: The Asian Experience* (1996).

BOOKS (recent publications): V.R. Panchamukhi, V.L. Rao & Nagesh Kumar, *Indo-Sri Lanka Economic Cooperation - An Operational Programme* (1993); Raj Sharma, *The "Missing Middle" in Sub-Saharan Africa: Role of South-South Cooperation* (1993); Ignacy Sachs, *Transition Strategies Towards the 21st Century* (1993); V.R. Panchamukhi, R.G. Nambiar, Rajesh Mehta, G.A. Tadas & S.R. Mohanty, *Complementarity in Trade and Production - Intra-South Potentials* (1995); V.R. Panchamukhi & Rehman Sobhan (eds.), *Towards An Asian Economic Area* (1995); R. Mehta & S.N. Sahay, *Industrial Growth and Technological Change - A Case Study of Selected Developing Countries* (1996); V.R. Panchamukhi, G.A. Tadas & S.K. Mohanty, *Basic Needs Issues in Development* (1997); V.R. Panchamukhi, V.L:. Rao & R. Upendra Das, *Trade and Industrial Development in South Asia* (1997).

Members

Dr. V.R. PANCHAMUKHI (Director)
Dr. V.L. RAO (Senior Fellow)
Dr. Biswajit DHAR (Fellow)
Dr. Rajesh MEHTA (Fellow)

Ms. Raj SHARMA (Senior Consultant)
Mr. R. Upendra DAS (Research Associate)
Mr. S.K. MOHANTY (Research Associate)
Ms. Priya BANERJEE (Research Assistant)
Dr. Sachin CHATURVEDI (Research Assistant)
Ms. Beena PANDEY (Research Assistant)
Mr. U.S. RANA (Research Assistant)
Mr. Saikat SINHA ROY (Research Assistant)

SCHOOL OF INTERNATIONAL STUDIES (SIS) JAWAHARLAL NEHRU UNIVERSITY

NEW MEHRAULI ROAD
NEW DELHI - 110 067
India
(91-11) 610 76 76, ext. 276/407
(91-11) 11 616 58 86, 616 22 92

Year of Creation
1969 (formerly *Indian School of International Studies*, created in 1955).

Publications
JOURNAL: *International Studies* (quarterly journal of SIS (1, 1959-).

Dean
Dr. Zafar IMAM

CENTRE FOR AMERICAN AND WEST EUROPEAN STUDIES
S.I.S., J.N.U.

NEW MEHRAULI ROAD
NEW DELHI - 110 067
India
☎ (91-11) 610 76 76, 610 75 57
(91-11) 616 58 86, 616 22 92

Research Orientations of Institute
Politics, economics and foreign policy dimensions of Western Europe, the United States and Latin America.

Areas of Expertise
International Politics and Diplomacy, Defence and Strategic Studies.

Regional Scope
Western Europe, Latin America, North America, South Asia.

Activities
Research Programmes, Conferences & Seminars, Exchange Programmes with other institutions, Documentation Centre (European Union Documentation Centre).

Members
Dr. Christopher Sam RAJ (Chairperson and Professor)
Dr. R.P. KAUSHIK (Professor)
Dr. R. NARAYANAN (Professor)
Dr. B. VIVEKANANDAN (Professor)
Dr. Rajendra K. JAIN (Associate Professor)
Dr. Abdul NAFEY (Associate Professor)
Dr. J.L. FERREIRA, Jr. (Assistant Professor)
Dr. (Ms.) K.P. Vijay LAKSHMI (Assistant Professor)

CENTRE FOR DIPLOMACY, INTERNATIONAL LAW & ECONOMICS S.I.S., J.N.U.

NEW MEHRAULI ROAD
NEW DELHI - 110 067
India
(91-11) 610 76 76, 610 75 57
(91-11) 616 58 86, 616 22 92

Research Orientations of Institute
M.Phil. and doctoral research in diplomacy, law and economics with emphasis on the global economics and polity.

Areas of Expertise
International Politics and Diplomacy, International Economics, International Law.

Regional Scope
Global.

Activities
Research Programmes, Conferences & Seminars, Exchange Programmes with other institutions, Library, Documentation Centre.

Members
Dr. Sandwip K. DAS (Chairperson & Professor)
Dr. Manmohan AGARWALA (Professor)
Dr. Ram Prakash ANAND (Professor)
Dr. Ashok GUHA (Professor)
Dr. K.D. KAPUR (Professor)
Dr. Rahamatullah KHAN (Professor)
Dr. Pushpesh PANT (Professor)
Dr. Yogesh TYAGI (Professor)
Dr. Alokesh BARUA (Associate Professor)
Dr. B.S. CHIMNI (Associate Professor)
Dr. Vijay JAMBHOLKAR (Associate Professor)
Dr. Manoj PANT (Associate Professor)
Dr. Amit ROY (Associate Professor)
Dr. Bharat DESAI (Assistant Professor)

CENTRE FOR EAST ASIAN STUDIES
S.I.S., J.N.U.

NEW MEHRAULI ROAD
NEW DELHI - 110 067
India
(91-11) 610 76 76 ext 2346
(91-11) 616 58 86, 616 22 92
rkrishna@jnuniv.ernet.in

Areas of Expertise
Japanese studies, Chinese studies, Korean studies.

Regional Scope
East Asia, South Asia.

Activities
Research Programmes, Conferences & Seminars, Exchange Programmes with other institutions, Library, Documentation Centre.

Members
Dr. R.R. KRISHNAN (Chairperson & Professor)
Dr. G.P. DESHPANDE (Professor)
Dr. K.V. KESAVAN (Professor)
Dr. P.A.N. MURTHY (Professor)
Dr. (Ms.) Lalima VARMA (Associate Professor)
Dr. (Ms.) Alka ACHARYA (Assistant Professor)
Dr. (Ms.) Madhu BHALLA (Assistant Professor)
Dr. H.S. PRABHAKAR (Assistant Professor)
Mr. Varaprasad SEKAR (Assistant Professor)

CENTRE FOR INTERNATIONAL POLITICS, ORGANIZATION & DISARMAMENT, S.I.S., J.N.U.

NEW MEHRAULI ROAD
NEW DELHI - 110 067
India
(91-11) 610 76 76 ext. 287/420
(91-11) 616 58 86, 616 22 92

Research Orientations of Institute
To promote studies in International Politics, Organization, Disarmament and Political Geography.

Areas of Expertise
International Politics and Diplomacy, Defence and Strategic Studies.

Regional Scope
Global.

Activities
Research Programmes, Conferences & Seminars, Library.

Members
Dr. K.S. JAWATKAR (Chairperson & Associate Professor)
Dr. Sushil KUMAR (Professor)
Dr. (Ms.) Surjit MANSINGH (Professor)
Dr. R.C. SHARMA (Professor)
Dr. Amitabh MATTOO (Associate Professor)
Dr. Varun SAHNI (Associate Professor)
Dr. C.S.R. MURTHY (Assistant Professor)

CENTRE FOR RUSSIAN, CENTRAL ASIAN & EAST EUROPEAN STUDIES S.I.S., J.N.U.

NEW MEHRAULI ROAD
NEW DELHI - 110 067
India
(91-11) 610 76 76 ext. 2365
(91-11) 616 58 86, 616 22 92

Areas of Expertise
International Politics and Diplomacy.

Regional Scope
Russia (+ Eastern Europe), Central Asia, South Asia.

Activities
Research Programmes, Conferences & Seminars, Exchange Programmes with other institutions, Documentation Centre.

Members
Dr. (Ms.) Nirmala JOSHI (Chairperson & Professor)
Dr. Zafar IMAM (Professor)
Dr. Devendra KAUSHIK (Professor)
Dr. Arvind VYAS (Professor)
Dr. (Ms.) Anuradha M. CHENOY (Associate Professor)
Dr. Shashi Kant JHA (Associate Professor)
Dr. Ajay PATNAIK (Associate Professor)
Dr. TULSIRAM (Associate Professor)
Dr. Shams-UD-DIN (Associate Professor)
Dr. Tahir ASGHAR (Assistant Professor)

CENTRE FOR SOUTH, CENTRAL, SOUTHEAST ASIAN & SOUTHWEST PACIFIC STUDIES
S.I.S., J.N.U.

✉ NEW MEHRAULI ROAD
NEW DELHI - 110 067
India
☎ (91-11) 610 76 76, ext. 276/407
📠 (91-11) 616 58 86, 616 22 92

Research Orientations of Institute
Interdisciplinary research on South Asian Studies.

Areas of Expertise
International Policy and Diplomacy, Defence and Strategic Studies, International Economics, South Asian History, Politics and Economics.

Regional Scope
Central Asia, South Asia, Southeast Asia, Southwest Pacific.

Activities
Research Programmes, Conferences & Seminars, Library, Documentation Centre (Urmila Phadnis Reference Unit).

Publications
JOURNALS: *South Asian Survey* (bi-annual published under the auspices of the *Indian Council for South Asian Cooperation*, 1, 1994-), *Himalayan and Central Asian Studies* (quarterly published under the auspices of the *Himalayan Research and Cultural Foundation* (*HRCF*), (1, 1997-).

Members
Dr. Indra Nath MUKHERJI (Chairperson & Professor)
Dr. Kalim BAHADUR (Professor)
Dr. Muchkund DUBEY (Professor)
Dr. (Ms.) Nancy JETLY (Professor)
Dr. S.D. MUNI (Professor)

Dr. Dawa NORBU (Professor)
Dr. Khulbhusan WARIKOO (Professor)
Dr. Shukla Ranjan CHAKRAVARTY (Associate Professor)
Dr. Mahendra P. LAMA (Associate Professor)
Dr. P. SAHADEVAN (Associate Professor)
Dr. (Ms.) Shyamali GHOSH (Research Officer)
Dr. Kapileshwar LABH (Research Officer)

CENTRE FOR WEST ASIAN AND AFRICAN STUDIES S.I.S., J.N.U.

NEW MEHRAULI ROAD
NEW DELHI - 110 067
India
☎ (91-11) 616 75 57
(91-11) 616 58 86

Areas of Expertise
International Policy and Diplomacy, Defence and Strategic Studies, International Economics.

Regional Scope
Africa, West Asia, South Asia.

Activities
Research Programmes, Conferences & Seminars, Exchange Programmes with other institutions, Documentation Centre, Teaching at Masters and above degrees.

Members
Dr. Girijesh PANT (Chairperson and Professor)
Dr. (Ms.) Gulshan DIETL (Professor)
Dr. Ajay DUBEY (Associate Professor)
Dr. A.K. PASHA (Associate Professor)
Dr. S.K. MALAKAR (Associate Professor)
Dr. P.C. JAIN (Assistant Professor)
Mr. A.K. MAHOPATRA (Assistant Professor)

SOUTH ASIAN CENTRE FOR STRATEGIC STUDIES (SACSS)

A-39 SOUTH EXTENSION - I
NEW DELHI - 110 049
India
(91-11) 469 88 86
(91-11) 464 99 96
cpsnd@del2.vsnl.net.in

Year of Creation
1996

Research Orientations of Institute
Autonomous research organisation engaged in the study and research on strategic issues with a focus on South Asia.

Areas of Expertise
Defence and Strategic Studies.

Regional Scope
South Asia.

Activities
Research Programmes, Conferences & Seminars, Documentation Centre.

Publications
JOURNALS: *Strategic Bulletin* (bi-monthly, 1, 1996-), *South Asia Watch* (monthly, 1, 1997-).

MONOGRAPHS: Occasionally.

Members
Dr. Riaz PUNJABI (Director & Professor)
Ms. Sreeradha DATTA (Coordinator & Research Associate)
Dr. Ashok K. BEHURIA (Research Associate)
Dr. Saleem KIDWAI (Editorial Advisor)
Dr. Kalim BAHADUR (Chairman, Research Advisory Council)

CENTRE FOR STRATEGIC STUDIES ALIGARH MUSLIM UNIVERSITY

✉ SARFRAZ HOUSE, UNIVERSITY ROAD
ALIGARH - 202 002
India
☎ (91-571) 400 921 ext. 187
(91-571) 400 105

Year of Creation
1988

Research Orientations of Institute
Defence and Strategic aspects of International Relations, Arms Control, Regional Security.

Areas of Expertise
International Politics and Diplomacy, Defence and Strategic Studies, International Economics, International Law.

Regional Scope
Western Europe, West Asia, Central Asia, South Asia.

Activities
Research Programmes (Ph.D. level), Conferences & Seminars, Exchange Programmes with other institutions, Library, Documentation Centre.

Publications
JOURNAL: *Strategic Studies Journal* (annual since 1988).

Members
Dr. Akhtar MAJEED (Director & Professor)
Dr. Salim AKHTAR (Professor)
Dr. Jawaid IQBAL (Assistant Professor)
Dr. Irshad PERVEZ (Assistant Professor)
Dr. Iqbalur REHMAN (Assistant Professor)

CENTRE OF WEST ASIAN STUDIES
ALIGARH MUSLIM UNIVERSITY

SARFRAZ HOUSE, UNIVERSITY ROAD
ALIGARH - 202 002
India
☎ (91-571) 400 921 ext. 198
(91-571) 400 105

Year of Creation
1967

Research Orientations of Institute
West Asia: History, Resources, Society, Languages, Domestic and International Politics.

Areas of Expertise
International Politics and Diplomacy, International Economics.

Regional Scope
West Asia.

Activities
Research Programmes (Ph.D. level), Conferences & Seminars, Exchange Programmes with other institutions, Library, Documentation Centre.

Publications
JOURNAL: *Journal of West Asian Studies* (annual since 1976).

Members
Dr. Akhtar MAJEED (Director & Professor)
Dr. Mehmoodur Rehman NADVI (Professor)
Dr. Nazim ALI (Associate Professor)
Dr. Mohammad GULRAZ (Associate Professor)
Dr. Shamir HASAN (Associate Professor)
Dr. Hasan Askari KAZMI (Associate Professor)

DEPARTMENT OF INTERNATIONAL RELATIONS
JADAVPUR UNIVERSITY

✉ CALCUTTA - 700 032
India
☎ (91-33) 473 61 94, extn. 10
📠 (91-33) 473 14 84

Year of Creation
1956

Research Orientations of Institute
International Political Economy, Regional Integration, Maritime Laws, Environmental Diplomacy, Refugee Studies, Theory Building in International Relations.

Areas of Expertise
International Politics and Diplomacy, Defence and Strategic Studies, International Economics, International Law.

Regional Scope
Western Europe, Russia (+ Eastern Europe), North America, West Asia, South Asia, Southeast Asia.

Activities
Research Programmes, Conferences & Seminars, Exchange Programmes with other institutions, Library, Documentation Centre.

Publications
JOURNAL: *Jadavpur Journal of International Relations* (annual).

Members
Dr. Gautam Kumar BASU (Head of Department & Professor)
Dr. Arun Kumar BANERJEE (Professor)
Dr. Jyotirmoy BANERJEE (Professor)
Dr. (Ms.) Malabika BANERJEE (Reader)
Dr. Purusottom BHATTACHARYA (Reader)

Dr. (Ms.). Sanjukta BHATTACHARYA (Reader)
Dr. (Ms.) Debi CHATTERJEE (Reader)
Dr. (Ms.) Anjali GHOSH (Reader)
Dr. (Ms.) Sucheta GHOSH (Reader)
Mr. Omprakash MISHRA (Reader)
Mr. R.L. RODRIGUES (Reader)
Dr. (Ms.) Purabi ROY (Reader)
Mr. Rabindra SEN (Reader)
Ms. Anuradha MUKHERJEE (Senior Lecturer)
Mr. Tridib CHAKRABORTY (Lecturer)
Ms. Kana CHATTERJEE (Lecturer)
Ms. Rochana DAS (Lecturer)
Dr. Anindya Jyoti MAZUMDAR (Lecturer)
Dr. (Ms.) Sumita SEN (Lecturer)

DEPARTMENT OF SOUTH AND SOUTHEAST ASIAN STUDIES UNIVERSITY OF CALCUTTA

✉ 51/1 HAZRA ROAD,
LAW BUILDING, 2nd Floor,
CALCUTTA - 700 091
India
☎ (91-33) 475 88 95
Fax (91-33) 241 32 22

Year of Creation
1978

Research Orientations of Institute
Undertake and promote analytical studies on major socio-economic, political-administrative and regional issues of common concern in South and Southeast Asia.

Areas of Expertise
International Politics and Diplomacy, International Economics, Population Studies, Burmese and Thai Language Teaching.

Regional Scope
South Asia, Southeast Asia.

Activities
Research Programmes, Conferences & Seminars, Exchange Programmes with other institutions, Documentation Centre, Language Training Programmes.

Publications
JOURNAL: *South and Southeast Asian Journal* (quarterly).

Members
Dr. Rajagopal Dhar CHAKRABORTI (Head of Department & Professor)
Dr. Buddhadev CHOUDHURY (Professor)

Dr. Ashish ROY (Professor)
Dr. Parimal GHOSH (Reader)
Dr. Swarna BHATTACHARYA (Senior Lecturer)
Dr. Subhendu DASGUPTA (Senior Lecturer)
Dr. (Ms.) Lipi GHOSH (Senior Lecturer)

MAULANA ABDUL KALAM AZAD INSTITUTE OF ASIAN STUDIES

567, DIAMOND HARBOUR ROAD (2nd & 3rd Floors)
BEHALA,
CALCUTTA - 700 034
India
(91-33) 468 13 96, 468 46 34
(91-33) 468 13 96
makaias@cal.vsnl.net.in

Year of Creation
1993

Research Orientations of Institute
The MAKA Institute of Asian Studies is a centre for research and learning with focus on social, cultural, political and economic movements in Asia from the middle of the nineteenth century onwards, with special emphasis on their links with India.

Areas of Expertise
International Politics and Diplomacy, Defence and Strategic Studies, Transcultural Studies, Immigration Studies.

Regional Scope
West Asia, Central Asia, South Asia.

Activities
Research Programmes (Governance, Immigration and Borders, Peace Studies), Conferences & Seminars, Exchange Programmes with other institutions, Library, Documentation Centre.

Publications
JOURNAL: Quarterly Newsletter.

MONOGRAPHS: Occasionally.

REPORTS: *Azad Institute Papers*.

Members
Dr. Barun DÉ (Director and Professor)
Dr. Ranabir SAMADDAR (Professor in charge)
Ms. Anita SENGUPTA (Research Associate)
Dr. Mohammed TAJUDDIN (Research Associate)
Ms. Abanti ADHIKARI (Research Scholar)

CENTRE FOR LATIN AMERICAN STUDIES UNIVERSITY OF GOA

S.P.O. TALEIGAO PLATEAU
BAMBOLIM - 403 205
India
(91-832) 221 347
(91-832) 224 184

Year of Creation
1988

Research Orientations of Institute
Interdisciplinary studies on Latin America.

Areas of Expertise
International Politics and Diplomacy, Defence and Strategic Studies, International Economics, International Law.

Regional Scope
Latin America, North America.

Activities
Research Programmes, Conferences & Seminars, Exchange Programmes with other institutions, Documentation Centre.

Publications
REPORTS: Research Reports.

Members
Dr. V. SHIVKUMAR (Director & Professor)
Mr. Dilip LOUNDO (Lecturer)
Mr. PUSHKAR (Lecturer)
Ms. Archana KAKODKAR (Librarian, Documentation Officer)

CENTRE FOR AREA STUDIES (URBAN DEVELOPMENT AND REGIONAL PLANNING IN THE INDIAN OCEAN REGION)

PRESS ROAD, OSMANIA UNIVERSITY
HYDERABAD - 500 007
Andhra Pradesh
India
(91-40) 701 89 51, 701 89 86 extn. 328

Year of Creation
1983

Research Orientations of Institute
Indian Ocean studies.

Areas of Expertise
International Politics and Diplomacy, Defence and Strategic Studies, International Economics, Regional Planning, Marine Resources, Environment.

Regional Scope
Africa, West Asia, South Asia, Southeast Asia.

Activities
Research Programmes, Conferences & Seminars, Library, Documentation Centre.

Publications
JOURNAL: Bi-annual Newsletter.

MONOGRAPHS: V. Yoga Joytsna, *Geo-Politics of Southern Africa and Problems of Land-Locked Countries*; Manisha Mookherjee, *Population Growth and Structure in Africa*; Geeta Reddy, *Agriculture in Zimbabwe*; Sheela Prasad, *Levels of Development in Zambia*; Channa Basavaiah Madapathi, *Political Economy of Marine Fisheries of India*.

Members

Dr. Rama MELKOTE (Director & Professor)
Mr. Venkateshwar P. RAO (Professor)
Dr. (Ms.) Sheela PRASAD (Lecturer)
Mr. Gautam MURTHY (Faculty Member)
Mr. Balakishan ANUMALLA (Lecturer in Geography)
Mr. Narayana BANALA (Lecturer in Economics)
Mr. Channa Basavaiah MADAPATHI (Lecturer in Political Science)
Ms. Manisha MOOKHERJEE (Lecturer in Sociology)
Ms. Geeta REDDY (Lecturer in Geography)

DEPARTMENT OF POLITICAL SCIENCE UNIVERSITY OF HYDERABAD

HYDERABAD - 500 046
Andhra Pradesh
India
(91-40) 301 05 00 extn. 3200
U@hyd.ernet.in

Year of Creation
1974

Research Orientations of Institute
International Relations including area studies, particularly Sub-Saharan Africa, South Asia, Russia and West Asia.

Areas of Expertise
International Politics and Diplomacy.

Regional Scope
Western Europe, Russia (+ Eastern Europe), Latin America, Africa, West Asia, South Asia, Southeast Asia, East Asia.

Activities
Research Programmes (Special Assistance Programme for International Relations under the U.G.C.), Library, Organisation of lectures by Indian and foreign scholars.

Publications
MONOGRAPHS: Occasional Papers.

Members
Dr. Rajendra HARSHE (Professor, Coordinator of Special Assistance Programme in International Relations Studies)
Dr. G. HARAGOPAL (Professor)
Dr. (Ms.) Shanta SINHA (Professor)
Dr. M. Mauzzam ALI (Associate Professor)

Dr. P. EASHVARAIAH (Associate Professor)
Dr. Sudhir Jacob GEORGE (Associate Professor)
Dr. P. MANIKYAMBA (Associate Professor)
Dr. Prakash C. SARANGI (Associate Professor)
Dr. Sanjay PABHIKUR (Associate Professor)
Dr. G. SUDERSHANAM (Associate Professor)
Dr. I. RAMABRAMHAM (Assistant Professor)

SOUTH ASIA STUDIES CENTRE (SASC)
UNIVERSITY OF RAJASTHAN

JAIPUR - 302 004
India
☎ (91-141) 511 175

Year of Creation
1963

Research Orientations of Institute
Multi-disciplinary research institution devoted to the study of India's neighbouring countries covering historico-cultural, socio-economic and political aspects.

Areas of Expertise
International Politics and Diplomacy, Domestics Politics of the South Asian Countries.

Regional Scope
West Asia, Central Asia, South Asia.

Activities
Research Programmes, Conferences & Seminars, Exchange Programmes with other institutions, Library, Documentation Centre.

Publications
JOURNAL: *South Asian Studies* (bi-annual, 1, 1966-).

BOOKS (recent publications): Alok Mathur, *The Two Nation Theory: A Study in the Context of Identity Crisis in Pakistan* (1994); Ramakant & P.L. Bhola, *Post-Cold War Developments in South Asia* (1995); M.L. Sharma, *Transnational Firms in Drug Industry in South Asia* (1995); S.N. Kaushik, *Ahmadiya Community in Pakistan: Travail, Discrimination and Alienation* (1996); Ramakant & R.C. Misra, *Bhutan: Society and Polity* (1996).

Members
Dr. Mohan Lal SHARMA (Director & Associate Professor)
Dr. R.C. MISHRA (Associate Professor)

Dr. (Ms.) Olive PEACOCK (Associate Professor)
Dr. Karori SINGH (Associate Professor)
Dr. B.C. UPRETI (Associate Professor)
Dr. P.L. BHOLA (Assistant Professor)
Dr. Surendra Nath KAUSHIK (Assistant Professor)
Dr. Shashi UPADHYAYA (Research Associate)
Dr. Krishan GOPAL (Research Associate)

CENTRE FOR CENTRAL EURASIAN STUDIES
UNIVERSITY OF MUMBAI

VIDYANAGARI, SANTACRUZ (E)
MUMBAI- 400 098
India
(91-22) 611 30 91
(91-22) 612 57 11

Year of Creation
1972

Research Orientations of the Institute
The Centre is basically an interdisciplinary research centre on the former Soviet States. It runs academic programmes at M.A. and Ph.D. levels on Central Eurasian Studies and research on socio-economic development, foreign policy, ethno-nationalism and economic development related to this area.

Areas of Expertise
International Politics and Diplomacy, Defence and Strategic Studies, International Economics.

Regional Scope
Russia (+ Eastern Europe), Central Asia, South Asia.

Activities
Conferences & Seminars, Documentation Centre.

Publications
JOURNALS: Newsletter and Bulletin.

REPORTS: Occasionally.

Members
Dr. Padma Lochan DASH (Director)
Dr. (Ms.) Vasundhara MOHAN (Reader)

Ms. Shoba GAEKWAD (Russian Lecturer)
Dr. (Ms.) Navsikha DUARA (Lecturer)
Dr. Sanjay DESHPANDE (Research Associate)
Dr. (Ms.) Rama Sampath KUMAR (Research Associate)

SCHOOL OF INTERNATIONAL STUDIES
UNIVERSITY OF PONDICHERRY

UNIVERSITY CAMPUS
R. VENKATARAMAN NAGAR, KALAPET
PONDICHERRY - 605 014
India
(91-413) 65177 ext. 333
(91-413) 65265 / 65211
biopu@pondiuni.ren.nic.in

Year of Creation
1988

Research Orientations of Institute
International Relations, India's Foreign Policy, South Asian, American and French Studies, Theories of International Politics.

Areas of Expertise
International Politics and Diplomacy, Defence and Strategic Studies.

Regional Scope
Western Europe, North America, South Asia.

Activities
Research Programmes (at M.Phil./Ph.D. levels), Conferences & Seminars, Library.

Publications
JOURNAL: Newsletter (bi-monthly).

MONOGRAPHS: Monographs on the Indian Ocean.

Members
Dr. S. GABRIEL (Dean in charge)
Dr. Nalini Kant JHA (Associate Professor)
Dr. B. KRISHNAMURTHY (Assistant Professor)
Mr. L. Prem SEKHARA

CENTRE OF CENTRAL ASIAN STUDIES (CCAS) UNIVERSITY OF KASHMIR

HAZRATBAL
SRINAGAR - 190 006
JAMMU AND KASHMIR
India
(91-194) 452 078, 452 405, Ext. 365
(91-194) 452 357, attention CCAS
@-qadri.ukash.ernet.in

Year of Creation
1978

Research Orientations of Institute
To comprehend the nature of multidimensional relations of Central Asian countries with the world in general and the contiguous countries in particular and to delineate and identify the specific areas of cultural facets.

Areas of Expertise
International Politics and Diplomacy, International Economics, History, Philosophy and Religion, Sociology, Languages.

Regional Scope
Central Asia (Afghanistan, Kazakhstan, Kyrghyzstan, Mongolia, North Eastern Iran, North Western Pakistan, Northern India, Tajikistan, Tibet, Turkmenistan, Uzbekistan, Xinjiang).

Activities
Research Programmes, Conferences & Seminars, Exchange Programmes with other institutions, Library, Documentation Centre.

Publications
JOURNALS: *Journal of Central Asian Studies* (annual, 1, 1989-), Newsletter.

Members

Dr. Abdul Majid MATTOO (Director & Professor, History)
Dr. Darakshan ABDULLAH (Lecturer, History)
Mr. Tareak AHMAD (Lecturer, Sociology)
Dr. (Ms.) Naseema AKHTAR (Lecturer, Political Science/International Relations)
Mr. Aijaz Ahmad BANDAY (Lecturer, Archaeology)
Dr G.N. KHAKI (Lecturer, Islamic Studies)
Dr. Rafi-ud-Din MAKHDOOMI (Lecturer, Mongolian Studies)
Dr. Gh. Mohi-ud-Din MIR (Lecturer, Geography)
Dr. Mohamad Afzal MIR (Lecturer, Economics)
Dr. Firdous TABASSUM (Lecturer, International Studies)
Mr. J.L. BHAN (Reader, Museology)
Dr. G.R. JAN (Reader, Persian)
Dr. Mushtaq Ahmad KAW (Reader, History)
Mr. Gulshan MAJID (Reader, Kashmiri)
Mr. Syed Reyaz RUFAI (Documentation Officer)

CENTRE FOR STUDIES ON INDOCHINA
SRI VENKATESHWARA UNIVERSITY

✉ TIRUPATI - 517 502
Andhra Pradesh
India
☎ (91-8574) 22467
Fax (91-8574) 27499

Year of Creation
1976

Research Orientations of Institute
To promote interdisciplinary study and research on the States of Indochina and to develop a comprehensive data base relating to Indochinese States.

Areas of Expertise
International Politics and Diplomacy, Defence and Strategic Studies.

Regional Scope
Southeast Asia, East Asia, Southwest Pacific.

Activities
Research Programmes, Conferences & Seminars, Exchange Programmes with other institutions, Library, Documentation Centre.

Publications
JOURNAL: *Indochina Review* (quarterly, 1, 1986-).

MONOGRAPHS: L.L. Mehrotra, *India's Contribution to the Peace Process in Cambodia* (1996); *Cambodia: The Paris Agreement and After* (1996); *Strategic Challenges to Indian Foreign Policy in the Aftermath of the Cold War* (1996).

Members
Dr. Arangam Lakshmana CHETTY (Director & Professor)
Dr. Konapalli Raja REDDY (Reader)

Dr. Yadamuri Yagama REDDY (Reader)
Mr. Chenna Reddy Ravindranatha REDDY (Lecturer)
Dr. Putta Munirathnam REDDY (Lecturer)

CENTRE FOR THE STUDY OF NEPAL
FACULTY OF SOCIAL SCIENCES
BANARAS HINDU UNIVERSITY

VARANASI - 221 005
Uttar Pradesh
India
☎ (91-542) 316 678

Year of Creation
1976

Research Orientations of Institute
Country Studies of Nepal and Bhutan.

Areas of Expertise
International Politics and Diplomacy, Defence and Strategic Studies, Multi-Disciplinary Approach.

Regional Scope
South Asia.

Activities
Research Programmes, Conferences & Seminars, Academic collaboration with Nepalese and other Himalayan research centres.

Publications
JOURNAL: *Indian Journal of Nepalese Studies* (bi-annual).

REPORTS: Occasionally.

MONOGRAPHS: *News and Views on Nepal*, *Occasional Paper Series.*

Members
Dr. Murlidhar DHARAMDASANI (Director)
Dr. (Ms.) V. SHARMA (Lecturer, Nepali Language)

OTHER INSTITUTIONS

CENTRE FOR THE STUDY OF GEOPOLITICS,
DEPARTMENT OF POLITICAL SCIENCE,
PUNJAB UNIVERSITY
SECTOR 14 CHANDIGARH - 160 014 (India)

DEPARTMENT OF DEFENCE STUDIES,
UNIVERSITY OF CHENNAI
CENTENARY BUILDINGS
CHEPAUK, TRIPLICANE
CHENNAI - 600 005 (India)

CENTRE FOR SOUTH AND SOUTHEAST ASIAN STUDIES,
UNIVERSITY OF CHENNAI
CENTENARY BUILDINGS
CHEPAUK, TRIPLICANE
CHENNAI - 600 005 (India)

DEPARTMENT OF CHINESE AND JAPANESE STUDIES,
UNIVERSITY OF DELHI
DELHI - 110 007 (India)

CENTRE FOR AFRICAN STUDIES,
UNIVERSITY OF MUMBAI
VIDYANAGARI, SANTACRUZ (E)
MUMBAI - 400 098 (India)

DEPARTMENT OF DEFENCE AND STRATEGIC STUDIES,
UNIVERSITY OF POONA
ARTS FACULTY BUILDING
UNIVERSITY OF POONA
PUNE - 411 007 (India)

CENTRE FOR SOUTH ASIAN STUDIES,
COLLEGE OF ARTS, COMMERCE AND LAW
ANDHRA UNIVERSITY
WALTAIR
VISAKHAPATNAM - 530 003 (India)

NEPAL

KATHMANDU

CENTRAL DEPARTMENT OF POLITICAL SCIENCE, TRIBHUVAN UNIVERSITY

CENTRE FOR NEPAL AND ASIAN STUDIES (CNAS), TRIBHUVAN UNIVERSITY

NEPAL COUNCIL OF WORLD AFFAIRS (NCWA)

CENTRE FOR ECONOMIC DEVELOPMENT AND ADMINISTRATION (CEDA), TRIBHUVAN UNIVERSITY

DEPARTMENT OF HISTORY, TRIBHUVAN UNIVERSITY

NEPAL CENTRE FOR CONTEMPORARY STUDIES

CENTRAL DEPARTMENT OF POLITICAL SCIENCE TRIBHUVAN UNIVERSITY

KIRTIPUR
KATHMANDU
Nepal
☎ (977-1) 226 964

Year of Creation
1961

Areas of Expertise
International Politics and Diplomacy, Defence and Strategic Studies, International Economics, International Law.

Regional Scope
Western Europe, Russia (+ Eastern Europe), Africa, West Asia, Central Asia, South Asia, Southeast Asia, East Asia, Southwest Pacific.

Activities
Research Programmes, Conferences & Seminars, Central Library (Tribhuvan University).

Publications
JOURNAL: *Nepalese Journal of Political Science.*

Members
Dr. Tribhuvan Nath JAISWAL (Head of Department & Professor)
Dr. Lok Raj BARAL (Professor)
Dr. Jitendra Dhoj KHAND (Professor)
Dr. Panna Kaji AMATYA (Associate Professor)
Dr. Shyam Kishore SINGH (Associate Professor)
Mr. Krishna Prasad KHANAL (Associate Professor)
Mr. Sridhar KHATRI (Associate Professor)

CENTRE FOR NEPAL AND ASIAN STUDIES (CNAS) TRIBHUVAN UNIVERSITY

✉ P.O. Box 3757, KIRTIPUR
KATHMANDU
Nepal
☎ (977-1) 227 184

Year of Creation
1972

Research Orientations of Institute
Nepal Studies and Social Sciences.

Regional Scope
South Asia.

Activities
Research Programmes, Conferences & Seminars, Exchange Programmes with other institutions, Library, Documentation Centre.

Publications
JOURNAL: *Contributions to Nepalese Studies* (1, 1973-, bi-annual since 1988).

BOOKS: Occasionally.

Members
Dr. Prem Kumar KHATRY (Director)
Dr. Prayag Raj SHARMA (Professor)
Mr. Dilli Ram DAHAL (Reader)
Ms. Subhadra Subba DAHAL (Reader)
Mr. Novel Kishore RAI (Reader)
Mr. Drone P. RAJAURE (Reader)
Mr. Ananda P. SHRESTHA (Reader)
Dr. Tek Bahadur SHRESTHA (Reader)
Mr. Dev Raj DAHAL (Lecturer)

Mr. Ramesh DHUNGEL (Lecturer)
Mr. Krishna HACHHETHU (Lecturer)
Mr. Mohan KHANAL (Lecturer)
Mr. Pramod KANTHA (Lecturer)
Ms. Sushila MANANDAR (Lecturer)
Mr. Dilli Raj SHARMA (Lecturer)
Mr. Dhruba Kumar SHRESTHA (Lecturer)
Mr. Nirmal Man TULADHAR (Lecturer)
Mr. Shree Krishna YADAV (Lecturer)
Ms. Prabha KAINI (Assistant Lecturer)
Mr. Nani Ram KHATRI (Assistant Lecturer)
Mr. Pancha Narayan MAHARAJAN (Assistant Lecturer)
Mr. Bal Gopal SHRESTHA (Assistant Lecturer)

NEPAL COUNCIL OF WORLD AFFAIRS (NCWA)

NCWA BUILDING, HARIHAR BHAVAN
PULCHOWK, LALITPUR, P.O. Box 2588
KATHMANDU
Nepal
☎ (977-1) 526 222

Year of Creation
1948

Research Orientations of Institute
Contribution to peace by promoting mutual cooperation among the nations of the world, and to act as an information centre of world events.

Areas of Expertise
International Politics and Diplomacy, Defence and Strategic Studies, International Law.

Regional Scope
Western Europe, Russia (+ Eastern Europe), North America, Africa, West Asia, South Asia, East Asia, Southwest Pacific.

Activities
Exchange Programmes with other institutions, Library, Documentation Centre.

Publications
JOURNAL: Annual Journal.

REPORTS: Occasionally.

Members
Dr. Soorya Lal AMATYA (President / Professor)
Mr. Khagendra Prasad BHATTARAI (General Secretary / Lecturer)
Dr. Panna Kaji AMATYA (Assistant Professor)
Mr. Surendra Bahadur SHRESTHA (Professor / Former Nepalese Ambassador)

Mr. Sworga MANSINGH SHRESTHA (Reader)
Ms. Madhuri SHRESTHA (Lecturer)
Mr. Birendra SHRESTHA (Former President)
Dr. Ananta Raj POUDYAL (Associate Professor)
Mr. Mridula SINGH KARMACHARYA (Associate Professor)
Mr. Gauri Rana JOSHI (Executive Member / Principal MMHSS)
Mr. Lakshman Bahadur KHATRI CHETRI (Executive Member / Lecturer)
Mr. Rishikesh SHAHA (President HURON / President NSHC)

OTHER INSTITUTIONS

CENTRE FOR ECONOMIC DEVELOPMENT AND ADMINISTRATION (CEDA), TRIBHUVAN UNIVERSITY

CEDA BUILDING
P.O. Box 3757, KIRTIPUR
KATHMANDU
(977-1) 213 325

Research Orientations : The CEDA focuses its research on planning, fiscal policy, rural development, population studies, human resources and management systems.

Publications

JOURNAL: *Journal of Development and Administrative Studies* (bi-annual).
REPORTS: Occasional Papers.

DEPARTMENT OF HISTORY, TRIBHUVAN UNIVERSITY

P.O. Box 3757, KIRTIPUR
KATHMANDU (Nepal)

NEPAL CENTRE FOR CONTEMPORARY STUDIES

P.O. Box 3316
KATHMANDU (Nepal)
(977-1) 521 522
(977-1) 419 385

PAKISTAN

ISLAMABAD

DEPARTMENT OF INTERNATIONAL RELATIONS, QUAID-I-AZAM UNIVERSITY

HUMAN DEVELOPMENT CENTRE (HDC)

INSTITUTE OF REGIONAL STUDIES (IRS)

INSTITUTE OF STRATEGIC STUDIES (ISS)

PAKISTAN INSTITUTE OF DEVELOPMENT ECONOMICS (PIDE)

DEPARTMENT OF DEFENCE AND STRATEGIC STUDIES, QUAID-I-AZAM UNIVERSITY

DEPARTMENT OF HISTORY, QUAID-I-AZAM UNIVERSITY

JAMSHORO

DEPARTMENT OF INTERNATIONAL RELATIONS, UNIVERSITY OF SINDH

FAR EAST AND SOUTH EAST ASIA STUDY CENTRE, UNIVERSITY OF SINDH

KARACHI

DEPARTMENT OF INTERNATIONAL RELATIONS, UNIVERSITY OF KARACHI

DEPARTMENT OF POLITICAL SCIENCE, UNIVERSITY OF KARACHI

PAKISTAN INSTITUTE OF INTERNATIONAL AFFAIRS (PIIA)

LAHORE

CENTRE FOR SOUTH ASIAN STUDIES (CSAS), UNIVERSITY OF THE PUNJAB

DEPARTMENT OF HISTORY, UNIVERSITY OF THE PUNJAB

PESHAWAR

AREA STUDY CENTRE - CENTRAL ASIA, UNIVERSITY OF PESHAWAR

QUETTA

AREA STUDY CENTRE - MIDDLE EAST, UNIVERSITY OF BALUCHISTAN

DEPARTMENT OF INTERNATIONAL RELATIONS QUAID-I-AZAM UNIVERSITY

ISLAMABAD
Pakistan
(92-51) 829 391
(92-51) 821 397
ismat@aun.sdnpk.undp.org

Year of Creation
1973

Areas of Expertise
International Politics and Diplomacy, Defence and Strategic Studies, International Economics, International Law.

Regional Scope
Africa, West Asia, Central Asia, South Asia.

Activities
Research Programmes, Conferences & Seminars, Exchange Programmes with other institutions, Library, Documentation Centre.

Members
Dr. Ijaz HUSSAIN (Chairman & Professor)
Dr. (Ms.) Lubna ABID ALI (Assistant Professor)
Dr. Raja EHSAN AZIZ (Assistant Professor)
Dr. Mahmood HASSAN BUTT (Assistant Professor)
Dr. Jeleconnais Rifaat HUSSAIN (Assistant Professor)
Dr. Syed Rifaat HUSSAIN (Assistant Professor)
Dr. (Ms.) Aqila KHAWAJA (Assistant Professor)
Dr. (Ms.) Rukhsana SIDDIQUI (Associate Professor)
Mr. Imran HAMEED (Lecturer)
Mr. Naseem RIZVI (Lecturer)
Ms. Ayesha ZULFIQAR (Lecturer)

HUMAN DEVELOPMENT CENTRE (HDC)

8, BAZAR ROAD
G-6/4
ISLAMABAD
Pakistan
(92-51) 201 114, 201 192
(92-51) 271 256
kh@hdc.sdnpk.undp.org

Year of Creation
1995

Research Orientations of Institute
Development economics with a focus on SAARC countries.

Areas of Expertise
Defence and Strategic Studies, International Economics, Human Development and Social Issues.

Regional Scope
South Asia.

Activities
Research Programmes, Conferences & Seminars.

Publications
REPORT: Mahbub ul Haq, *Human Development in South Asia 1997*.

Members
Dr. Mahbub ul HAQ (Founder)
Ms. Salma MASUD (Senior Policy Analyst)
Mr. Ali MAHDI (Senior Policy Analyst)
Mr. Hyat TAIMUR (Senior Policy Analyst)
Ms. Masooda BANO (Research Fellow)
Mr. Adeel MALIK (Research Fellow)
Ms. Sadia MALIK (Research Fellow)
Mr. Richard PONZIO (Visiting Research Fellow)

INSTITUTE OF REGIONAL STUDIES (IRS)

NAFDEC COMPLEX, F-56, BLUE AREA
NAZIMUDDIN ROAD, F-6/1
ISLAMABAD
Pakistan
☎ (92-51) 920 39 74
(92-51) 920 40 55
aziz@irspak.sdnpk.undp.org

Year of Creation
1982

Research Orientations of Institute
The Institute of Regional Studies is an independant, non-profit scholarly research centre devoted to the objective study of the region that Pakistan is situated in.

Areas of Expertise
International Politics and Diplomacy, Defence and Strategic Studies, International Economics.

Regional Scope
South Asia, West Asia, Central Asia and Indian Ocean community.

Activities
Research Programmes, Exchange Programmes with other institutions, Library, Documentation Centre.

Publications
JOURNALS : *Regional Studies* (quarterly, 1, 1982-), *Spotlight on Regional Affairs* (monthly), *Selections from Regional Press* (fortnightly).

REPORTS: *Regional Perspective*, *Focus on Regional Issues.*

MONOGRAPHS: *Monographs Series - Regional.*

BOOKS (recent publications): *Great Powers and South Asia: Post-Cold War Trends; The State of Muslims in India; Pakistan and Regional*

Economic Cooperation in SAARC-ECO; Afghanistan: Past, Present and Future; Central Asia: Internal & External Dynamics.

Members

Lt. Gen. Nishat AHMAD (Retd.) (Director)
Brigadier Bashir AHMAD (Retd.) (Senior Fellow)
Dr. Khalid MAHMOOD (Professor & Research Associate)
Dr. Ghani JAFFAR (Research Associate)
Dr. Maqsudul Hasan NURI (Research Associate)
Dr. (Ms.) Farhat PERVEEN (Research Associate)
Dr. Abul Barakat AHMAD (Editor)
Mr. Mohammad IQBAL
Ms. Shaheen AKHTAR
Ms. Amera SAEED
Mr. Khalid Mahmood MALIK

INSTITUTE OF STRATEGIC STUDIES (ISS)

P.O. Box 1173
SECTOR F-5/2
ISLAMABAD
Pakistan
(92-51) 920 44 23, 920 44 24, 920 24 41
(92-51) 920 46 58

Year of Creation
1973

Research Orientations of Institute
Research is both area and issue oriented. It includes South, Central and West Asia, the Asia-Pacific Region, CIS, Europe, the US, arms control, nuclear non-proliferation, the new world order, etc.

Areas of Expertise
International Politics and Diplomacy, Defence and Strategic Studies.

Regional Scope
Western Europe, North America, West Asia, Central Asia, South Asia, Southeast Asia, East Asia, Southwest Pacific.

Activities
Research Programmes, Conferences & Seminars, Exchange of scholars and publications, Library, Documentation Centre.

Publications
JOURNALS: *Strategic Studies* (quarterly, 1, 1978-), *Strategic Perspectives* (quarterly).

REPORTS: *Afghanistan Reports*, Reports on Central Asia, India, Japan and Kashmir.

MONOGRAPHS: *Islamabad Papers.*

Members
Dr. Agha Murtaza POOYA (Director)
Dr. Suroosh IRFANI (Senior Research Fellow)

Dr. Ghani JAFAR (Senior Research Fellow)
Dr. (Ms.) Fahmida ASHRAF (Research Fellow)
Dr. Mahrukh KHATTAK (Research Fellow)
Dr. Najam RAFIQUE (Research Fellow)
Dr. Fazal-UR-RAHMAN (Research Fellow)

PAKISTAN INSTITUTE OF DEVELOPMENT ECONOMICS (PIDE)

P.O. Box 1091
ISLAMABAD - 44000
Pakistan
☎ (92-51) 812 440
(92-51) 210 886

Year of Creation
1957

Research Orientations of Institute
Fundamental research on economics and in-service training in economic analysis, research methods and project evaluation.

Areas of Expertise
Development economics and Islamic economics in general and Pakistan's economic problems in particular.

Activities
Research Programmes, Library, Documentation Centre.

Publications
JOURNAL: *The Pakistan Development Review* (quarterly, 1, 1962-).

REPORTS: *PIDE Tidings* (thrice a year).

MONOGRAPHS (recent publications): *Essays in Islamic Economic Philosophy*, *Essays in Development Economics.*

Members
Dr. Syed Nawab Haider NAQVI (Director & Professor)
Dr. Faiz BILQUES
Dr. Nadeem Akhtar BURNEY
Dr. Ziaul HAQUE
Mr. Zafar IQBAL
Dr. A.R. KEMAL
Dr. Ashfaque Hasan KHAN

Mr. Riaz MAHMOOD
Dr. Zafar MAHMOOD
Dr. Safraz KHAN QURESHI
Mr. Shamim Ara SAHIBZADA
Dr. Khwaja SARMAD
Dr. Tayyeb SHABBIR

DEPARTMENT OF INTERNATIONAL RELATIONS UNIVERSITY OF SINDH

JAMSHORO
(SINDH)
Pakistan
☎ (92-221) 771 575

Year of Creation
1972

Areas of Expertise
International Politics and Diplomacy, Defence and Strategic Studies, International Economics, International Law.

Regional Scope
West Asia, Central Asia, South Asia, East Asia.

Activities
Research Programmes, Conferences & Seminars, Exchange Programmes with other institutions, Library, Documentation Centre.

Members
Dr. Mehtab Ali SHAH (Chairman & Professor)
Dr. M.I.S. Bukhari SHAH (Professor)
Ms. Perveen AFRIDI (Associate Professor)
Mr. A.K. CHACHER (Associate Professor)
Dr. Lutfullah MARGI (Associate Professor)
Mr. Pervaiz H. MIRZA (Associate Professor)
Ms. Azra KANDHAR (Assistant Professor)
Mr. Abdul Hakim LAKHO (Assistant Professor)
Ms. Naghma MANGHRIO (Assistant Professor)
Mr. Abdul Latif TUNJIO (Assistant Professor)
Mr. Sheikh INAM (Lecturer)

DEPARTMENT OF INTERNATIONAL RELATIONS UNIVERSITY OF KARACHI

UNIVERSITY CAMPUS
KARACHI 75270
Pakistan
☎ (92-21) 479 001-7 Extn. 2274
(92-21) 496 33 73 - 496 31 24

Year of Creation
1958

Research Orientations of Institute
Most of the research is on conflict building measures and on the three regions mentioned below.

Areas of Expertise
International Politics and Diplomacy, Defence and Strategic Studies.

Regional Scope
Middle East, South Asia, Central Asia.

Activities
Research Programmes, Conferences & Seminars.

Members
Dr. Talat A. WIZARAT (Director & Professor)
Dr. Syed Sikander MEHDI (Professor)
Mr. Moonis AHMAR (Associate Professor)
Ms. Khalida GHOUS (Associate Professor)
Mr. Khalid MAHMOOD (Associate Professor)
Mr. Mutahir AHMED (Lecturer)
Ms. Sheila Z. AHMED (Lecturer)
Ms. Huma Naz SIDDIQUI (Lecturer)
Ms. Shaista TABASSUM (Lecturer)

CENTRE FOR SOUTH ASIAN STUDIES (CSAS) UNIVERSITY OF THE PUNJAB

✉ QUAID-I-AZAM CAMPUS
LAHORE - 54590
Pakistan
☎ (92-42) 586 40 14
(92-42) 586 72 06

Year of Creation
1973

Research Orientations of Institute
The CSAS sets out to extend and improve public understanding of socio-economic and political developments in South Asia.

Areas of Expertise
International Politics and Diplomacy, Defence and Strategic Studies, Social Developments.

Regional Scope
South Asia.

Activities
Research Programmes, Conferences & Seminars, Exchange Programmes with other institutions, Library, Documentation Cell.

Publications

JOURNALS: *CSAS Newsletter*, *South Asian Studies* (bi-annual, 1, 1984-).

REPORTS: *Seminar Papers*, *South Asia Papers*, *South Asian Minority Affairs*.

MONOGRAPHS: *Research Aid Series*, *Country Information Series*.

BOOKS: Occasionally.

Members

Dr. Sarfaraz Hussain MIRZA (Director & Professor)
Dr. Rafique AHMAD (Advisor)
Dr. Aslam QURESHI (Literary Editor & Professor)
Mr. Mohammad Jahangir TAMEMI (Associate Professor)
Mr. Asghar ALI (Research Officer)
Ms. Musarrat CHEEMA (Research Officer)
Mr. Abdul MAJEED (Research Officer)

DEPARTMENT OF HISTORY
UNIVERSITY OF THE PUNJAB

✉ NEW CAMPUS
LAHORE
Pakistan
☎ (92-42) 586 39 83

Year of Creation
1882

Areas of Expertise
International Politics and Diplomacy.

Regional Scope
Western Europe, North America, Central Asia, South Asia.

Activities
Research Programmes, Conferences & Seminars, Library, Documentation Centre.

Publications
JOURNAL: *Journal of the Punjab Historical Society* (1, 1911-).

Member
Dr. Sadiq Ali GILL (Chairman & Professor)

AREA STUDY CENTRE - CENTRAL ASIA UNIVERSITY OF PESHAWAR

PESHAWAR
(N.W.F.P.)
Pakistan
☎ (92-521) 41327

Year of Creation
1976

Research Orientations of Institute
Political and economic studies on contemporary Central Asia.

Areas of Expertise
International Politics and Diplomacy, Defence and Strategic Studies, International Economics.

Regional Scope
Central Asia.

Activities
Research Programmes, Conferences & Seminars, Exchange Programmes with other institutions, Library, Documentation Centre.

Publications
JOURNAL: *Central Asia* (bi-annual).

BOOKS: *Muslim Celebrities of Central Asia*; *Afghanistan Today*; *The Ruling Dynasties of Central Asia*; *The Geo-Political Imperatives of Pakistan*; *A History of Science, Technology and Culture in Central Asia* (vol.1); *Zakhira-e-Khwarazmshahi* (Urdu); *Khamkhana-i-Yasrab* (Persian); *Devan-i-Rahmat Davi* (Pushtu).

Members
Dr. Azmat HAYAT KHAN (Director)
Dr. Pervez IQBAL KHAN (Assistant Professor)

Dr. Khalil SAEED (Assistant Professor)
Mr. Abdullah JAN KHALIL (Associate Professor)
Mr. Mohammad ABDULLAH (Research Associate)
Mr. Sarfraz KHAN (Research Associate)

OTHER INSTITUTIONS

DEPARTMENT OF DEFENCE AND STRATEGIC STUDIES, QUAID-I-AZAM UNIVERSITY

✉ QUAID-I-AZAM UNIVERSITY CAMPUS
P.O. Box 1091
ISLAMABAD - 44000 (Pakistan)

DEPARTMENT OF HISTORY, QUAID-I-AZAM UNIVERSITY

✉ QUAID-I-AZAM UNIVERSITY CAMPUS
P.O. Box 1091
ISLAMABAD - 44000 (Pakistan)

FAR EAST AND SOUTH EAST ASIA STUDY CENTRE, UNIVERSITY OF SINDH

✉ JAMSHORO
DISTRICT DADU (Pakistan)

DEPARTMENT OF POLITICAL SCIENCE, UNIVERSITY OF KARACHI

✉ UNIVERSITY CAMPUS
KARACHI (Pakistan)

PAKISTAN INSTITUTE OF INTERNATIONAL AFFAIRS (PIIA)

✉ AIWAN-E-SADAR ROAD
P.O. Box 1447
KARACHI - 74200 (Pakistan)
☎ (92-21) 568 28 91

Research Orientations: Created in 1947, the PIIA is dedicated to the promotion of scientific studies on international politics, Pakistan foreign policy, economics and jurisprudence.

Publications

JOURNAL: *Pakistan Horizon* (quarterly).
MONOGRAPHS: Occasionally.
BOOKS: Occasionally.

AREA STUDY CENTRE - MIDDLE EAST,
UNIVERSITY OF BALUCHISTAN
SARIAB ROAD
QUETTA (Pakistan)

SRI LANKA

COLOMBO

BANDARANAIKE CENTRE FOR INTERNATIONAL STUDIES (BCIS)

BANDARANAIKE INTERNATIONAL DIPLOMATIC TRAINING INSTITUTE (BIDTI)

CENTRE FOR POLICY RESEARCH AND ANALYSIS (CEPRA)

DEPARTMENT OF HISTORY AND POLITICAL SCIENCE, UNIVERSITY OF COLOMBO

INSTITUTE OF POLICY STUDIES (IPS)

INTERNATIONAL CENTRE FOR ETHNIC STUDIES (ICES)

MARGA INSTITUTE

REGIONAL CENTRE FOR STRATEGIC STUDIES (RCSS)

KANDY / PERADENIYA

INSTITUTE OF INTERNATIONAL STUDIES (IIS)

DEPARTMENT OF HISTORY, PERADENIYA UNIVERSITY

DEPARTMENT OF POLITICAL SCIENCE, PERADENIYA UNIVERSITY

BANDARANAIKE CENTRE FOR INTERNATIONAL STUDIES (BCIS)

BMICH, BAUDDHALOKA MAWATHA
COLOMBO - 7
Sri Lanka
(94-1) 698 019
(94-1) 697 420

Year of Creation
1974

Areas of Expertise
International Politics and Diplomacy, Defence and Strategic Studies, International Economics, International Law, Languages (Sinhala, Tamil, Japanese and Chinese).

Regional Scope
Western Europe, Russia (+ Eastern Europe), Latin America, North America, Africa, West Asia, Central Asia, South Asia, Southeast Asia, East Asia, Southwest Pacific.

Activities
Research Programmes (India's Role in South Asia - 1991-92, International Political and Economic Changes after the Cold War - 1993-96), Conferences & Seminars, Library, Documentation Centre (United Nations depository), Regular diploma and postgraduate diploma programmes in International Affairs.

Publications
REPORTS: Summary Report - *SAARC : Problems and Prospects* (1991), Summary Report - *An Assessment of the Non-Aligned Movement* (1992), *SAARC: The Potential for Regional Security*, Convocation Booklet - 12th Convocation - *'Market-Friendly' Policies : An Appraisal.*

MONOGRAPHS: Occasional Papers.

BOOKS: Shelton U. Kodikara (ed.), *Dilemmas of Indo-Sri-Lankan Relations* (1991); Vernon L.B. Mendis (ed.), *India's Role in South*

Asia (1992); Bertram Bastiampallai (ed.), *India and Her South Asian Neighbours* (1992).

Member

Mr. Reginald (Ray) George Bernard FORBES (Director)

BANDARANAIKE INTERNATIONAL DIPLOMATIC TRAINING INSTITUTE (BIDTI)

SUITE 3G-07, BMICH
COLOMBO - 7
Sri Lanka
☎ (94-1) 682 109, 682 110, 682 111
(94-1) 436 630, 338 591

Year of Creation
1995

Areas of Expertise
International Politics and Diplomacy, Defence and Strategic Studies, International Economics, International Law.

Regional Scope
Western Europe, North America, Africa, West Asia, Central Asia, South Asia, Southeast Asia, East Asia, Southwest Pacific.

Activities
Research Programmes, Conferences & Seminars, Exchange Programmes with other institutions, Library, Documentation Centre, Continuous general course of lectures and special courses for diplomats.

Publications
JOURNAL: Bi-Monthly Newsletter.

Members
Dr. Vernon L.B. MENDIS (Director General)
Dr. Lorna S. DEWARAJA (Director)

CENTRE FOR POLICY RESEARCH AND ANALYSIS (CEPRA)

FACULTY OF LAW, UNIVERSITY OF COLOMBO
REID AVENUE
COLOMBO - 3
Sri Lanka
(94-1) 595 667
(94-1) 786 82 97
cepra@sri.lanka.net

Year of Creation
1993

Research Orientations of Institute
Conflict Management and Resolution, Legislative and Constitutional Reforms.

Areas of Expertise
International Politics and Diplomacy, Defence and Strategic Studies, International Law, HIV Law.

Regional Scope
South Asia, Southeast Asia, East Asia, Southwest Pacific.

Activities
Research Programmes, Conferences & Seminars, Library, Documentation Centre.

Publications
MONOGRAPHS: *Swiss Federation: Lessons for Sri Lanka*, Jayantha Gunaratne; *Centre-Provincial Relations in Canada: Lessons for Sri Lanka*, Robert Boron (Sinhala translation); *Essays on Constitutional Reforms*, Jayadeva Uyangoda & Rohan Edrisinha (eds.); *Introduction to Provincial Councils in Sri Lanka* , Shirani Bandaranayake & Tressie Leitan (Sinhala); *The CEPRA Oral History Transcripts*, Paikiasothy Saravanamuttu (ed.); *Documents on Media and Reporting on Conflict*, Jayadeva Uyangoda & Paikiasothy Saravanamuttu (eds.); *Sri*

Lanka: Lost Opportunities, Ketheeshwaran Loganathan; *Internal Refugees*, Mahesh Senanayake (Sinhala).

Members (Board of Management)
Dr. Jayadeva UYANGODA (Co-Director & Senior Lecturer, Department of History and Political Science)
Mr. Naganathan SELVAKKUMARAN (Co-Director & Senior Lecturer, Faculty of Law)
Dr. R.A. ARIYARATNE (Rector, Western Campus, University of Colombo)
Dr. Rohan EDRISINHA (Lecturer, Law)
Dr. Weligamage Don LAKSHMAN (Vice-Chancellor, Chairman)
Dr. (Ms.) Tressie LEITAN (Associate Professor, Department of History and Political Science)
Dr. Paikiasothy SARAVANAMUTTU (Research Consultant)

DEPARTMENT OF HISTORY AND POLITICAL SCIENCE UNIVERSITY OF COLOMBO

P.O. Box 1490
CUMARATUNGA MUNIDASA MAWATHA
COLOMBO - 3
Sri Lanka
(94-1) 500 474, 500 443
(94-1) 583 810

Year of Creation
1963

Areas of Expertise
International Politics and Diplomacy, Defence and Strategic Studies.

Regional Scope
South Asia.

Activities
Research Programmes, Conferences & Seminars, Documentation Centre.

Publications
JOURNAL: (with the Faculty of Law) *Sri Lanka Journal of International Law* (annual, 1, 1989-).

BOOK: S.U. Kodikara, *Indo-Sri Lanka Agreement of July 1987* (1989).

Members
Dr. M.G.A. COORAY (Head of Department, Associate Professor)
Dr. (Ms.) Indrani B. MUNASINGHE (Professor)
Dr. Amal JAYAWARDENA (Associate Professor)
Dr. W.M. KARUNADASA (Associate Professor)
Dr. (Ms.) Tressie LEITAN (Associate Professor)
Dr. (Ms.) Nayani MELEGODA (Senior Lecturer)
Dr. Jayadeva UYANGODA (Senior Lecturer)
Dr. (Ms.) Nira WICKRAMASINGHE (Senior Lecturer)

INSTITUTE OF POLICY STUDIES (IPS)

99, ST. MICHAEL'S ROAD
COLOMBO - 3
Sri Lanka
(94-1) 431 368, 431 378, 431 408
(94-1) 431 395
ips@sri.lanka.net

Year of Creation
1990

Research Orientations of Institute
Macro Policies, Agricultural Economics, Health Economics, International Economics, Education Economics, Industrial Economics, Public Enterprises Reforms, Environmental Economics, Labour Economics, Poverty and Income Distribution, Statistical and Computer Services.

Areas of Expertise
International Economics.

Regional Scope
Southeast Asia (Sri Lanka).

Activities
Research Programmes, Conferences & Seminars, Library, Documentation Centre.

Publications
REPORTS: *Research Studies: Macroeconomic Series*, *Governance Series*, *Industrialization Series*, *International Series*, *Macroeconomic Series*, *Working Papers*, etc.

Members
Dr. Saman KELEGAMA (Executive Director)
Dr. Wimal HETTIARACHCHI (Senior Visiting Fellow)
Dr. Shelton WANASINGHE (Senior Visiting Fellow)

Ms. Ramani GUNATILAKA (Research Economist)
Mr. Prematilake SAMARATNE (Research Economist)
Dr. Dushni WEERAKOON (Research Fellow)
Ms. Malathy KNIGHT-JOHN (Research Officer)
Mr. Jayaratne WEERASOORIYA (Project Officer)

INTERNATIONAL CENTRE FOR ETHNIC STUDIES (ICES)

2, KYNSEY TERRACE
COLOMBO - 8
Sri Lanka
☎ (94-1) 685 085
(94-1) 698 048
ices_cmb@sri.lanka.net

554/1, PERADENIYA ROAD
KANDY
Sri Lanka
☎ (94-8) 234 892
(94-8) 234 892
ices@slt.lk

Year of Creation
1982

Areas of expertise
International Politics and Diplomacy, International Law, Women's Studies.

Regional Scope
Western Europe, Russia (+ Eastern Europe), Latin America, North America, Africa, West Asia, Central Asia, South Asia, Southeast Asia, East Asia.

Activities
Research Programmes (1996/97: *Comparative Federalism, Democratic Transitions, Regional Co-operation and Conflict Resolution, Sri Lanka Governance Project, Comparative Electoral Processes in South Asia, Multiculturalism and Modes of Ethnic Coexistence in South and South East Asia, Violence against Women, The Causes of Conflict in Developing Countries, The Press and the Process of Democratization in South Asia, Participation of Women in Politics in South Asia, Ethnic Conflict Management and Resolution: International Experience and Lessons*

from Central Europe, Affirmative Action in South and South-East Asia, Administrative Arrangements for Implementing Devolution, Rebuilding War-Torn Societies), Conferences & Seminars, Exchange programmes with other institutions, Library, Documentation Centre.

Publications

JOURNALS: *Ethnic Studies Report* (bi-annual, 1, 1983-), *Nêthrâ* (quarterly, 1, 1996-).

REPORTS: Niaz Naik & Bradman Weerakoon, *Bhutan-Nepal Refugee Issue: A Report of a Fact-Finding Mission to Nepal* (1995); Devendra Raj Panday & Jeevan Thiagarajah, *Chittagong Hill Tracts: Displacement, Migrations, Accommodation: a Report* (1996)

MONOGRAPHS: *ICES Ethnic Studies Series*, *ICES Sri Lanka Studies Series*, *Monographs Series*, *ICES Occasional Paper Series*, *ICES Pamphlet Series*.

BOOKS (recent publications): Radhika Coomaraswamy, *Ideology and the Constitution: Essays on Constitutional Jurisprudence* (1996); K.M. de Silva, *Regional Powers and Small State Security: India and Sri Lanka, 1977-1990* (1996); Neelan Tiruchelvam, *Democracy and Human Rights* (Tamil, 1996); Report of the SAARC-NGO Observers; *Governance and the Electoral Process in Bangladesh, Parliamentary Elections* (1996); ICES, *Sri Lanka: The Devolution Debate* (3rd edn. 1997).

Members

Dr. (Ms.) Radhika COOMARASWAMY (Director - Colombo)
Dr. Neelan TIRUCHELVAM (Director - Colombo)
Dr. K.M. De SILVA (Executive Director - Kandy)
Dr. S.W.R. de A. SAMARASINGHE (Director - Kandy)
Dr. (Ms.) Yasmin TAMBIAH (Associate Director of Research Colombo)
Dr. (Ms.) Sirima KIRIBAMUNE (Senior Research Fellow - Kandy)
Dr. G.H. PEIRIS (Senior Research Fellow - Kandy)
Dr. K.N.O. DHARMADASA (Senior Research Fellow - Kandy)
Dr. Sunil BASTIAN (Research Fellow - Colombo)
Dr. Sasanka PERERA (Research Fellow - Colombo)
Dr. M. SOMASUNDARAM (Research Fellow - Colombo)
Dr. (Ms.) Darini RAJASINGHAM (Research Fellow - Colombo)

Dr. (Ms.) Nira WICKREMASINGHE (Research Fellow - Colombo)
Mr. THAMBIRAJAH (Librarian and Documentation Officer - Colombo)
Ms. Kanthi GAMAGE (Librarian and Documentation Officer - Kandy)

MARGA INSTITUTE

93/10, DUTUGEMUNU STREET
KIRILLAPONE
COLOMBO - 6
Sri Lanka
(94-1) 828 544, 829 013
(94-1) 828 597
marga@sri.lanka.net

Year of Creation
1972

Research Orientations of Institute
An independant non-governmental centre for development research in economic, social and political fields and related activities.

Areas of Expertise
International Economics, Developmental Research.

Regional Scope
South Asia, Southeast Asia.

Activities
Research Programmes, Conferences & Seminars, Exchange Programmes with other Institutions, Library, Documentation Centre maintaining an information system of socio-economic literature and statistics on SAARC countries.

Publications
JOURNALS: *Marga Quarterly Journal* (1, 1984-), *Marga Newsletter* (quarterly), Sinhala and Tamil Journals.

BOOKS (recent publications): *Devolution in a Multi-Ethnic Society*, *Collective Identities Revisited*; Sinhala medium and Tamil medium: *East Asian Miracle*, *Models of Democratic Government*, *Democratic Ideas*, *Democracy in a Plural Society*.

Members

Dr. G. USWATTE-ARATCHI (Executive Vice-Chairman)
Mr. Godfrey GUNATILLEKE (Chairman)
Ms. Myrtle PERERA (Director, Research)
Mr. D.H. SATHISCHANDRA (Associate Director, Research)

REGIONAL CENTRE FOR STRATEGIC STUDIES (RCSS)

2, ELI BANK ROAD
COLOMBO - 5
Sri Lanka
(94-1) 599 734-5
(94-1) 599 993
rcss@sri.lanka.net
website: http://www.lanka.net/rcss

Year of Creation
1992

Research Orientations of Institute
The RCSS is a South Asian forum for studies, training and multi-track dialogue and deliberation on issues of regional interest. All activities of RCSS are designed with a South Asia focus and are usually participated by experts from all South Asian countries. The Centre is envisaged as a forum for advancing the cause of co-operation, security, conflict resolution, confidence-building, peace and development in the countries of the South Asian region.

Areas of Expertise
International Politics and Diplomacy, Defence and Strategic, Confidence-building and Regional Cooperation in South Asia, Alternative thinking on issues and policies that affect the future of South Asia.

Regional Scope
South Asia.

Activities
Collaborative research and networking programmes involving individuals and institutions from all the South Asian countries, Conferences & Seminars, Research grants and other programmes specifically targetted at the younger generation of South Asian professionals.

Publications

JOURNAL: *RCSS Newsletter* (quarterly, 1, 1993-).

MONOGRAPHS: *RCSS Policy Studies* (Occasional, 1, 1997-); Nira Wickramasinghe, *Humanitarian Relief Organizations and Challenges to Sovereignty: The Case of Sri Lanka*; Stephen P. Cohen, *The Structural Dimensions of Conflict in South Asia.*

BOOKS: S.D. Muni & Lok Raj Baral (eds.), *Refugees and Regional Security in South Asia* (1996); P.R. Chari, Pervaiz Iqbal Cheema & Iftekharuzzaman (eds.), *Nuclear Non-proliferation in India and Pakistan: South Asian Perspectives* (1996); Iftekharuzzaman (ed.), *Regional Economic Trends and South Asian Security* (1997); Iftekharuzzaman (ed.), *Ethnicity and Constitutional Reforms in South Asia* (1997).

Members (International Research Committee)
Dr. IFTEKHARUZZAMAN (Director, RCSS)
Dr. (Ms.) Samina AHMED (Institute of Regional Studies, Islamabad)
Dr. R.A. ARIYARATNE (Rector, Horana Campus, University of Colombo)
Dr. Lok Raj BARAL (Professor of Political Science, Tribhuvan University, Kathmandu)
Dr. P.R. CHARI (Co-Director, Institute for Peace and Conflict Studies, New Delhi)
Dr. Pervaiz Iqbal CHEEMA (Professor of International Relations, Quaid-i-Azam University, Islamabad)
Dr. Stephen P. COHEN (Professor of Political Science, University of Illinois at Urbana-Champaign)
Mr. Dipak GYAWALI (Economist and Water Resources Engineer, Interdisciplinary Analysts, Kathmandu)
Dr. Abdur Rob KHAN (Research Director, BIISS, Dhaka)
Dr. Vernon L.B. MENDIS (Director General, Bandaranaike International Diplomatic Training Institute, Colombo)
Dr. S.D. MUNI (Professor, Appadorai Chair in International Political & Area Studies, JNU, New Delhi)
Dr. Robert O'NEILL (Chichele Professor of the History of War, All Souls College, University of Oxford)
Dr. Gowher RIZVI (Editor, *Contemporary South Asia*, Queen Elizabeth House, University of Oxford)
H.E. Mr. Ibrahim H. ZAKI (Minister for Tourism, Maldives, Former Secretary General of SAARC)

INSTITUTE FOR INTERNATIONAL STUDIES (IIS)

71, MULGAMPOLA ROAD
KANDY
Sri Lanka
☎ (94-8) 32738
(94-8) 32343

Year of Creation
1987

Research Orientations of Institute
International Affairs, Regional and National Economic Development and Politics.

Areas of Expertise
International Politics and Diplomacy, Defence and Strategic Studies, International Economics, Development Issues, Social Change and Political Protest.

Regional Scope
Western Europe, Russia (+ Eastern Europe), West Asia, South Asia, Southeast Asia, East Asia, Southwest Pacific.

Activities
Research Programmes, Conferences & Seminars, Exchange Programmes with other institutions, Library, Documentation Centre.

Publications
BOOKS: *Security Dilemma of a Small State*, vol. 1 (1992), vol. 2 (1995).

Members
Dr. Gamini Bandara KEERAWELLA (Director)
Dr. Ranjith AMARASINGHE (Professor)
Dr. Sivarajah AMBALAVANAR (Assistant Professor)
Dr. Pathira Vasam Jinasena JAYASEKERA (Assistant Professor)
Dr. Wijekoon Mudiyanselage TILAKARATNE (Senior Lecturer)

OTHER INSTITUTIONS

DEPARTMENT OF HISTORY, PERADENIYA UNIVERSITY
✉ UNIVERSITY PARK
PERADENIYA (Sri Lanka)

DEPARTMENT OF POLITICAL SCIENCE, PERADENIYA UNIVERSITY
✉ UNIVERSITY PARK
PERADENIYA (Sri Lanka)

GILLES BOQUÉRAT, member of the Centre d'Etudes de l'Inde et de l'Asie du Sud, is currently research fellow at the Centre de Sciences Humaines. He specializes in political and diplomatic history of contemporary South Asia.